Progress in Mathematics

MENTAL TESTS AND PHASE TESTS
FOR BOOK 2C

Les Murray BA

Senior Teacher and Head of Mathematics, Garstang County High School

Stanley Thornes (Publishers) Ltd

First published in 1985 by Stanley Thornes (Publishers) Ltd, Old Station Drive, Leckhampton, Cheltenham GL53 0DN, UK

British Library Cataloguing in Publication Data

Murray, L.
   Progress in mathematics.
   Book 2C Mental tests and phase tests
   1. Mathematics————1961–
   I. Title
   510   QA37.2
   ISBN 0-85950-270-8

Typeset by Grafikon Ltd, Oostkamp, Belgium.
Printed and bound in Great Britain by Ebenezer Baylis & Son, Worcester.

Mentai Tests

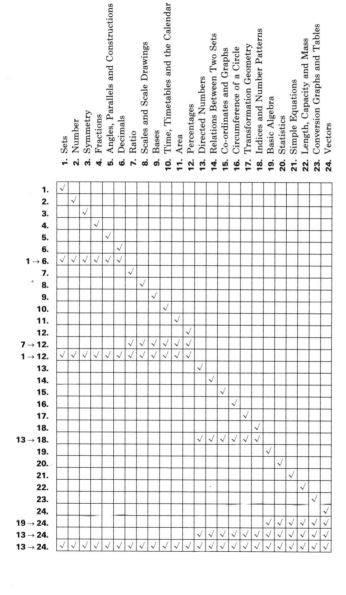

	1. Sets	2. Number	3. Symmetry	4. Fractions	5. Angles, Parallels and Constructions	6. Decimals	7. Ratio	8. Scales and Scale Drawings	9. Bases	10. Time, Timetables and the Calendar	11. Area	12. Percentages	13. Directed Numbers	14. Relations Between Two Sets	15. Co-ordinates and Graphs	16. Circumference of a Circle	17. Transformation Geometry	18. Indices and Number Patterns	19. Basic Algebra	20. Statistics	21. Simple Equations	22. Length, Capacity and Mass	23. Conversion Graphs and Tables	24. Vectors
1.	√																							
2.		√																						
3.			√																					
4.				√																				
5.					√																			
6.						√																		
1 → 6.	√	√	√	√	√	√																		
7.							√																	
8.								√																
9.									√															
10.										√														
11.											√													
12.												√												
7 → 12.							√	√	√	√	√	√												
1 → 12.	√	√	√	√	√	√	√	√	√	√	√	√												
13.													√											
14.														√										
15.															√									
16.																√								
17.																	√							
18.																		√						
13 → 18.													√	√	√	√	√	√						
19.																			√					
20.																				√				
21.																					√			
22.																						√		
23.																							√	
24.																								√
19 → 24.																			√	√	√	√	√	√
13 → 24.													√	√	√	√	√	√	√	√	√	√	√	√
13 → 24.	√	√	√	√	√	√	√	√	√	√	√	√	√	√	√	√	√	√	√	√	√	√	√	√

1. Which of these are simple closed curves?

    (a)   (b)   (c)   (d)   (e)

2. Show on a Venn diagram:
    (a) the set of even numbers less than 11.
    (b) the set of numbers that are less than 75 and divide exactly by 10.

3. List these sets using curly brackets and commas:
    (a) The set of letters in the word NUMBERS.
    (b) The set of odd numbers less than 15.

4. Copy and complete these sets:
    (a) The set of factors of 20 = {1, 2, ? , 5, ? , 20}

    (b) The set of prime numbers less than 20
        = {2, ? , 5, ? , ? , 13, ? , 19}

    (c) A set of quadrilaterals
        = {square, ? , kite, trapezium, ? , rhombus}

    (d) The set of multiples of 8 that are less than 80
        = {8, 16, ? , ? , 40, ? , 56, ? , ? }

5. From the given set, list:
    (a) the set of even numbers,
    (b) the set of numbers that divide exactly by 5.

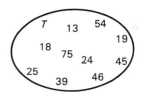

6. Here is a set of numbers: {4, 5, 6, 7, 10, 11, 14, 15}.
Write a set of numbers in which the members are twice as big as the members of the set above.

7. For each statement, write whether it is true or false:
    (a) 97 ∈ {odd numbers}   (c) ivy ∈ {plants}
    (b) 15 ∈ {prime numbers}

8. Which of these are empty sets?
   (*a*) {odd numbers that divide exactly by 10}
   (*b*) {even numbers that divide exactly by 5}

9. How many members has each of these sets?
   (*a*) {days of the week whose names begin with T}
   (*b*) {even numbers that lie between 15 and 31}

10. Find the sum of the set of
   numbers in:
   (*a*) the circle,
   (*b*) the parallelogram,
   (*c*) the square only.

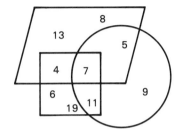

Mental Test 2 ═══════════════════ Number

1. Write the odd numbers that lie between 12 and 20.

2. Which is the smallest number of: 426, 398, 918, 981, 908, 627, 913, 819, 980?

3. Take 10 from 508.

4. Write 67 000 in words.

5. 41 thousand + 26 thousand.

6. What is the product of 9 and 4?

7. 6×2.

8. 60×20.

9. 10×43.

10. 36×1000.

3

11. 40 × 300.

12. Round 368 correct to the nearest hundred.

13. What is the sum of the digits of 863?

14. Does 8 × 4 = 15 + 18?

15. If 8 ⟨?⟩ 9 = 17, what is the missing sign, +, −, × or ÷?

16. A pen costs £3.78. How much change should I get out of £5?

17. My bus fare is 87 p per journey. What is the cost of two journeys?

18. Five people shared 37 cards equally. How many cards were left over?

19. Estimate the answer to 476 × 32.

20. Here is a set of numbers: {35, 45, 54, 60, 63, 75, 81}.
(a) Which numbers in the set divide exactly by 5?
(b) Which numbers in the set divide exactly by 9?

Mental Test 3 ━━━━━━━━━━━━━━━ Symmetry

1. Which of these shapes have bilateral symmetry?
(a)    (b)   (c)

2. Write two letters of the alphabet that have bilateral symmetry.

3. How many axes of bilateral symmetry, if any, has:
(a) a square?   (b) a parallelogram?   (c) a rectangle?

4

4. For each shape in question 1, write 'Yes' if it has rotational symmetry, otherwise write 'No'.

5. Write the names of two quadrilaterals that have rotational symmetry.

Mental Test 4 ━━━━━━━━━━━━━━━━━ Fractions

1. (*a*) What fraction is shaded?
(*b*) What fraction is unshaded?

2. ⬚ ? quarters make a whole.

3. Write in figures: three-fifths.

4. Write in words: $\frac{9}{10}$.

5. Write the numerator of the fraction $\frac{7}{12}$.

6. A cake is shared equally among eight people. What fraction does each person get?

7. $\dfrac{4}{8} = \dfrac{1}{\boxed{?}}$. Find the missing denominator.

8. Give the simplest equivalent fraction for $\frac{6}{8}$.

9. Which is bigger:
(*a*) $\frac{1}{4}$ or $\frac{1}{5}$?   (*b*) $\frac{3}{8}$ or $\frac{3}{7}$?   (*c*) $\frac{1}{3}$ or $\frac{1}{10}$?

10. Amit cut his piece of wood into eighths while Kim cut one of the same size into twelfths. Who had the bigger pieces?

11. How many eighths are there in 3?

12. How many sixths are there in $2\frac{5}{6}$?

13. Change $3\frac{1}{3}$ into an improper fraction.

14. Change $\frac{13}{5}$ into a mixed number.

15. Write 20 quarters as a whole number.

16. Find $\frac{1}{4}$ of 20 oranges.

17. Find $\frac{2}{3}$ of 18 cm.

18. Find $\frac{3}{4}$ of £1 in pence.

19. Carry out these calculations:

(a) $\dfrac{5}{10} + \dfrac{4}{10}$ (b) $3 \times \dfrac{2}{5}$ (c) $\dfrac{8}{9} - \dfrac{7}{9}$ (d) $1 - \dfrac{7}{12}$

20. Carry out these calculations. Simplify your answers.

(a) $\dfrac{5}{16} + \dfrac{7}{16}$ (b) $\dfrac{7}{12} - \dfrac{3}{12}$

Mental Test 5 ━━━━━━ Angles, Parallels and Constructions

1. Write whether each angle is an acute angle, an obtuse angle, a reflex angle or a right-angle:

(a)   (b)   (c)

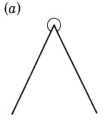 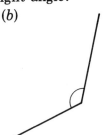 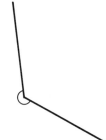

2. Write whether the given angle is an acute angle, an obtuse angle, a reflex angle or a right-angle:

(a) 125°   (b) 90°   (c) 310°   (d) 29°   (e) 270°

3. *Estimate* the size of each angle:

(a)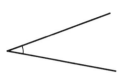

(b)

4. How many degrees are there in:

(a) $\frac{1}{2}$ turn?   (b) $\frac{1}{10}$ turn?

5. In the diagram, which angle has been marked, $\angle\,SQP$ or $\angle\,SQR$?

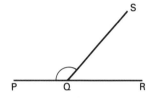

6. Copy and complete the sentence:
Angles on a straight line add up to $\boxed{?}\,°$.

7. *Calculate* the missing angles (labelled θ):

(a)

(b)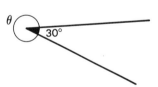

8. In the diagram:

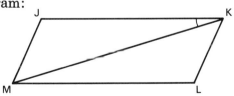

(a) Which angle has been marked, $\angle\,JKL$, $\angle\,JMK$, $\angle\,KJM$ or $\angle\,MKJ$?

(b) Which side is parallel to ML?

7

1. Write the value of the underlined digit.
   (Choose from: thousands, hundreds, tens, units, tenths, hundredths.)
   (a) 284.$\underline{7}$ (b) 6$\underline{3}$.1   (c) 965.2$\underline{8}$ (d) 1$\underline{4}$3.09

2. Change $\frac{7}{10}$ to a decimal.

3. Write $\frac{49}{100}$ as a decimal.

4. Write $2\frac{3}{10}$ as a decimal.

5. Write 7.8 correct to the nearest whole number.

6. Write 85.6 correct to the nearest whole number.

7. Write correct to one significant figure:
   (a) 61.2   (b) 4.9   (c) 2.56   (d) 853.6

8. Estimate the answer to 76.4 × 3.

9. Find the cost of 2 puzzles at 99 p each.

10. Find the cost of 2 posters at £1.99 each.

Mental Test 1 → 6 ════════════════════════════════════

1. Show on a Venn diagram the set of odd numbers that lie between 30 and 40.

2. Using curly brackets and commas, list the set of multiples of 4 that are less than 25.

3. How many members has the set of even numbers that are less than 35?

4. What is the product of 40 and 60?

5. Find the difference between 80 and 54.

6. Round 681 to the nearest hundred.

7. Estimate the answer to 49×72.

8. Here is a set of triangles:
{isosceles triangle, scalene triangle, equilateral triangle}.
(*a*) Which of the triangles have bilateral symmetry?
(*b*) Which of the triangles has rotational symmetry?

9. How many axes of bilateral symmetry has a rhombus?

10. Does a parallelogram have bilateral symmetry?

11. Which is bigger, $\frac{7}{10}$ or $\frac{7}{12}$?

12. How many quarters are there in $2\frac{3}{4}$?

13. What is $\frac{1}{3}$ of £21?

14. A bar of chocolate is shared equally among six people. What fraction does each person get?

15. (*a*) Is an angle of 149° an obtuse angle?
(*b*) Is an angle of 182° an obtuse angle?

16. How many degrees are there in:
(*a*) $\frac{1}{4}$ turn?　　　　　　　　(*b*) $\frac{3}{4}$ turn?

17. (*a*)　　　　　　　　　　　(*b*)

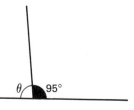

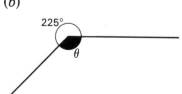

Angle θ = ⬚?　　　　　　　Angle θ = ⬚?

9

18. Write as a decimal:

(a) $\dfrac{9}{10}$

(b) $\dfrac{36}{100}$

(c) $\dfrac{1}{2}$

19. Write these decimals correct to the nearest whole number:

(a) 2.8   (b) 65.7   (c) 8.36   (d) 93.87

20. Estimate the answer to 6×47.5.

Mental Test 7 ━━━━━━━━━━━━━━━━━━━━━━ Ratio

1. A straight line is 13 cm long. How long is a straight line that is twice as long?

2. How many times bigger is the first quantity than the second?
(a) 15 min, 3 min   (b) £18, £6   (c) 28 km, 7 km

3. How many times longer is the first line than the second?

_____

_____

4. How many times bigger is the first quantity than the second?
(a) £1.50, 25 p   (c) 4 cm, 5 mm
(b) 2 years, 6 months

5. What fraction of the second quantity is the first?
(a) 5 h, 20 h   (b) 50 p, £3

6. Carol ran 400 m. Marios ran twice as far. How far was that?

Mental Test 8 ━━━━━━━━━━━ Scales and Scale Drawings

1. Using a scale of 1 cm to 2 m, what would be the true length of a line that is:
(a) 5 cm long?   (b) 9 cm long?   (c) 2.5 cm long?

2. Using a scale of 1 cm to 5 km, what would be the true length of a line that is:
 (*a*) 2 cm long?   (*b*) 7 cm long?   (*c*) 2.5 cm long?

3. Using a scale of 1 cm to 3 m, what length of line would you draw to show a line that is:
 (*a*) 9 m long?   (*b*) 15 m long?   (*c*) 24 m long?

4. Using a scale of 1 cm to 4 km, what length of line would you draw to show a distance of:
 (*a*) 16 km?   (*b*) 28 km?   (*c*) 14 km?

Mental Test 9 ════════════════════════════ Bases

1. Screws are in packs of eight. How many screws are there if there are:
 (*a*) 2 packs of screws?
 (*b*) 1 pack of screws and 3 left over?
 (*c*) 3 packs of screws and 2 left over?

2. Write these base 8 numbers in base ten:
 (*a*) 21_8 (*b*) 34_8 (*c*) 60_8

3. You pack screws in eights. How many packs can you make up and how many screws are left over if you have:
 (*a*) 20 screws?   (*b*) 14 screws?

4. Marbles are in packs of five. How many marbles are there if there are:
 (*a*) 2 packs of marbles?
 (*b*) 3 packs of marbles and 1 marble left over?
 (*c*) 2 packs of marbles and 3 marbles left over?

1. How many days are there in 2 weeks?

2. How many weeks are there in 35 days?

3. How many days are there in one week and five days?

4. There are 24 h in a day. How many hours are there in 2 days?

5. How many minutes are there in 3 h?

6. Change 120 min into hours.

7. Change 240 s into minutes.

8. How many seconds are there in 5 min?

9. How many minutes are there in 1 h 25 min?

10. Write 8.30 p.m. using the 24-hour clock.

11. What time is shown on the given clock face?
(It is morning.)
Give the time using the 24-hour clock.

12. Write 'twenty past three in the afternoon' using the 24-hour clock.

13. It is now 06.45. How many minutes are there to seven o'clock in the morning?

14. Ian arrived at the station 20 min early. His train was a quarter of an hour late. For how many minutes did he wait?

15. 25 March 1984 can be written as 25.3.84.
Write 6 August 1985 in figures.

Mental Test 11

1. How many small squares are
there in the rectangle shown?

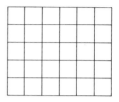

2. Calculate the area of a rectangle of length 9 cm and breadth
3 cm.

3. A rectangle of area 42 m² has a
breadth of 6 m. Calculate its
length.

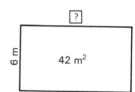

4. Find the area of a square with sides of 5 cm.

5. Calculate the area of the
parallelogram:

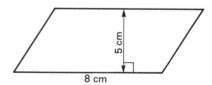

6. Calculate the area of the
triangle:

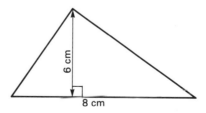

7. Calculate the area of a parallelogram with base 6 cm and
perpendicular height 3 cm.

8. Calculate the area of a triangle with base 5 cm and perpendicular height 6 cm.

13

Mental Test 12

1. What percentage of the large square has been shaded?

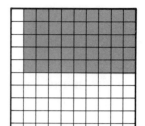

2. Write as percentages:
   (*a*) 84 out of 100
   (*b*) $\frac{32}{100}$

3. Change to common fractions:
   (*a*) 71%   (*b*) 19%   (*c*) 50%   (*d*) 25%   (*e*) 75%

4. Change to decimals:
   (*a*) 25%   (*b*) 65%   (*c*) 43%   (*d*) 8%

5. Find 50% of £18.

6. Find 25% of £32.

7. Find 75% of £24.

8. Find 50% of £27.50.

Mental Test 7 → 12

1. How many times bigger is the first quantity than the second?
   (*a*) 60 miles, 20 miles   (*b*) 36 p, 12 p   (*c*) 3 m, 50 cm

2. (*a*) What fraction of £18 is £6?
   (*b*) What fraction of 16 cm is 12 cm?

3. Using a scale of 1 cm to 6 km, what would be the true length of a line that is:
   (*a*) 2 cm long?   (*b*) 4 cm long?   (*c*) 5 cm long?

4. Using a scale of 1 cm to 10 m, what length of line would you draw to show a distance of:
(*a*) 20 m?   (*b*) 80 m?   (*c*) 30 m?

5. Five chocolate bars are sold in a pack. How many chocolate bars would I have bought if I bought:
(*a*) 3 packs?   (*b*) 1 pack and 3 extra bars?

6. Write these base 8 numbers in base ten:
(*a*) 17_8 (*b*) 31_8

7. If the 4 June is a Wednesday, what day is the 12 June of the same year?

8. It is now 10.25. How many minutes are there to 11 o'clock in the morning?

9. How many minutes are there in 2 h 10 min?

10. How many days are there in January?

11. Calculate the area of a parallelogram with base 7 m and perpendicular height 5 m.

12. A rectangle of area 40 cm^2 has a length of 10 cm. Find its breadth.

13. Calculate the area of a triangle with base 7 cm and perpendicular height 6 cm.

14. Change to decimals:
(*a*) 35%   (*b*) 96%   (*c*) 70%

15. Change to percentages:

(*a*) 15 out of 100   (*b*) $\dfrac{49}{100}$ (*c*) $\dfrac{92}{100}$

16. (*a*) Find 50% of £40.
(*b*) Find 25% of £14.
(*c*) Find 75% of £36.

1. Using curly brackets and commas, list the set of factors of 18.

2. Is {people whose birthday is on 31 November} an empty set?

3. How many digits has the number 760 431?

4. Round 4723 to the nearest thousand.

5. A tape costs £1.65. How much change should you get out of £5?

6. Here are some letters: {A, B, F, H, L, M, N, Z}.
  (*a*) Which of the letters have bilateral symmetry?
  (*b*) Which of the letters have rotational symmetry?
  (*c*) Which of the letters has both bilateral symmetry and rotational symmetry?

7. Find $\frac{1}{2}$ of £36.

8. Find $1 - \frac{7}{12}$.

9. Calculate the missing angles (labelled θ):
  (*a*)

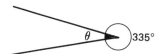
335°

  (*b*)

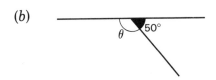
50°

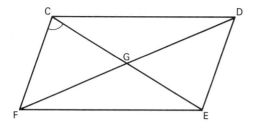

10. In the diagram:
   (a) Which angle has been marked, ∠ FCD, ∠ GCD, ∠ GCF or ∠ DCF?
   (b) Which side is parallel to CF?

11. Write $\frac{73}{100}$ as a decimal.

12. Write 4.7 correct to the nearest whole number.

13. (a) How many times as big as 6 yards is 30 yards?
   (b) What fraction of 12 km is 8 km?

14. Using a scale of 1 cm to 10 km, what would be the true length of a line that is:
   (a) 2 cm long?   (b) 5 cm long?   (c) 3 cm long?

15. Write these base 8 numbers in base ten:
   (a) 16_8 (b) 25_8

16. Write 'quarter past ten in the evening' using the 24-hour clock.

17. How many minutes are there in 1 h 50 min?

18. Calculate the area of a parallelogram with base 8 cm and perpendicular height 4 cm.

19. Change to decimals:
   (a) 52%   (b) 19%   (c) 85%

20. Find 25% of £20.

Mental Test 13 ═══════════ Directed Numbers

1. Is $^-15\,°C$ warmer than $^-20\,°C$?

2. Which is warmer, $^-7\,°C$ or $^-2\,°C$?

3. Which is colder, $4\,°C$ or $^-8\,°C$?

4. Which is colder, $^-4\,°C$ or $^-8\,°C$?

5. Here is a set of temperatures:
   $\{^-5\,°C,\ 8\,°C,\ 0\,°C,\ 2\,°C,\ ^-2\,°C,\ ^-7\,°C,\ 6\,°C\}$.
   (a) Which is the lowest temperature in the set?
   (b) Which member of the set is the highest temperature?
   (c) Which member of the set is the third lowest temperature?

6. Write whether the statements below are true or false:
   (a) $^-3 < ^-1$ (b) $^-7 > ^+4$ (c) $0 < ^-8$

7. Write these numbers in order of size. Put the largest first.
   (a) $^-7,\ ^+2,\ ^-9$ (b) $0,\ ^-10,\ ^-2$

8. An aeroplane was flying at 12 000 m. If it loses height by 4500 m, find its new height.

9. Answer these. Use the number line to help you.
   (a) $6 - 15$ (b) $^-9 - 4$ (c) $^-8 + 3 - 5 + 1$

10. The temperature is $^-2\,°C$. If the temperature now falls by $6\,°C$ what is the new temperature?

18

1. Answer these using the relation given:

(a) Who wears size 4 shoes?

(b) What size shoes does Dean wear?

(c) How many people wear size 3 shoes?

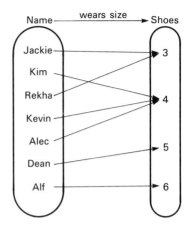

2. For the relation 'is 2 more than' only the first arrow has been drawn. It shows that 7 maps to 5.

(a) What does 4 map to?

(b) What does ⁻4 map to?

(c) What does 11 map to?

(d) What does 1 map to?

(e) What maps to 1?

(f) What maps to ⁻8?

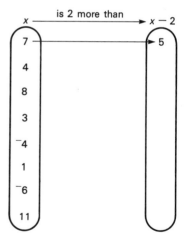

3. If $t = 4$ find the value of:

(a) $t + 7$ (b) $3t$ (c) $2t - 3$

4. Find the value of $m - 7$ when $m = 19$.

5. Find the value of $d + 3$ when $d = {}^-10$.

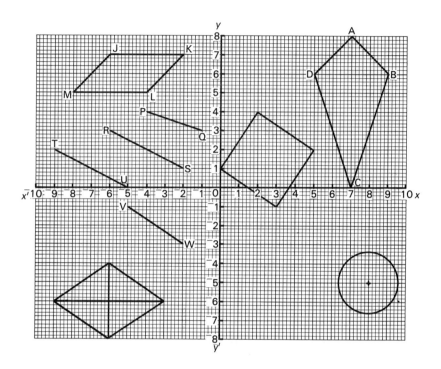

1. What are the co-ordinates of the four vertices of the square?

2. Which vertex of the kite is at $(5, 6)$?

3. What are the co-ordinates of the centre of the circle?

4. What are the co-ordinates of the origin?

5. What are the co-ordinates of the four vertices of the parallelogram?

6. Which line is parallel to TU?

7. What are the co-ordinates of vertex C on the kite?

8. Which point lies inside the circle, $(5, \,^-7)$ $(^-5, 7)$ $(7, \,^-5)$ or $(^-7, 5)$?

20

9. What are the co-ordinates of the point of intersection of the diagonals of the rhombus?

10. On which side of the parallelogram does the point ($^-7, 5$) lie?

Mental Test 16 ——————— Circumference of a Circle

1. What is the diameter of the circle shown?

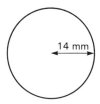

14 mm

2. The diameter of a circle is 12 cm. What is its radius?

3. A circle has a radius of 25 mm. Find its diameter.

4. What is the circumference of a circle with a diameter of 10 cm?

10 cm

5. What is the circumference of a circle of radius 7 cm?

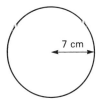

7 cm

6. What is the circumference of a circle of diameter 13 cm?

1. Write whether the transformation is a translation or a rotation:
   (a) the turning of the pages of a book
   (b) a stone dropped from a high tower
   (c) a drawer being closed

2. The black shaded L-shape has been transformed to positions A, B, C, D and E. List the letters A, B, C, D and E. Next to each one, write whether it shows a translation, a reflection or a rotation:

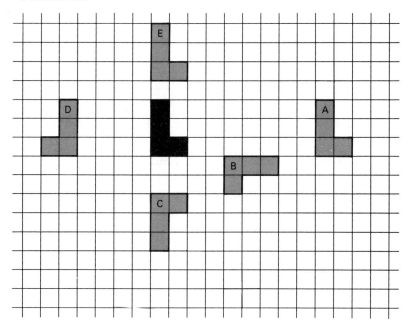

3. For each mapping, write whether it is true or false:
   (a)

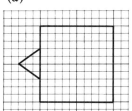 $\frac{1}{4}$ turn clockwise ⟶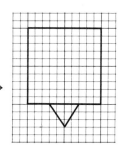

(b)

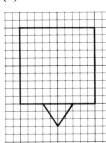
$\frac{1}{2}$ turn clockwise
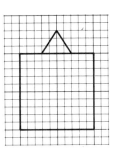

(c)

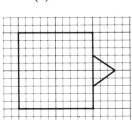
$\frac{1}{4}$ turn anticlockwise
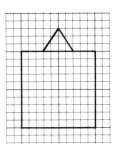

Mental Test 18 — Indices and Number Patterns

1. Write $c \times c \times c \times c$ in index form.

2. Find the value of:
   (a) 4^2 *(b)* 6^2 *(c)* 9^2 *(d)* 2^3

3. Find the value of n^4 when $n = 2$.

4. Here is a set of numbers:
   $\{2, 3, 4, 5, 6, 8, 9, 11, 15, 19, 25, 30, 36, 43, 45\}$.
   (a) Which numbers in the set are prime numbers?
   (b) Which numbers in the set are rectangular numbers?
   (c) Which numbers in the set are square numbers?
   (d) Which numbers in the set are triangular numbers?

5. Here is a sequence: 2, 9, 16, 23, 30, ?, ?, ...
   What are the two missing numbers?

1. Write these temperatures in order, from coldest to hottest:
$^-5\,°C$, $^+3\,°C$, $^-9\,°C$, $^-11\,°C$.

2. Write whether these are true or false:
    (a) $^-7 > ^-10$ (b) $^+2 < ^-15$ (c) $^-20 < ^-25$

3. Use the number line on p. 18 to help you with these:
    (a) $^-8 + 2$ (b) $^-6 - 4$ (c) $^+5 - 11$

4. Answer these using the
given relation:
    (a) What does 10 map to?
    (b) What does 8 map to?
    (c) What maps to 0?
    (d) What maps to 6?
    (e) What maps to $^-6$?
    (f) What does $^-4$ map to?

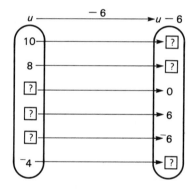

5. Using $k = 7$, find the value of:
    (a) $k + 8$
    (b) $k - 12$
    (c) $3k$
    (d) $2k - 5$

6. Use the shapes drawn on p. 25 to answer these:
    (a) The point (6, 8) is the centre of a shape.
        What is that shape called?
    (b) Give the co-ordinates of the vertices of the square.
    (c) What are the co-ordinates of the origin?
    (d) In the right-angled triangle, what are the co-ordinates of
        the vertex where the right-angle is?
    (e) Give the co-ordinates of the point of intersection of the
        diagonals of the parallelogram.

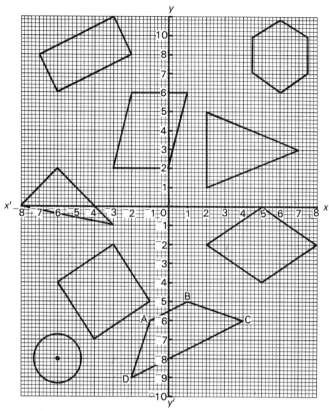

7. What is the circumference of a circle with a diameter of 4 cm?

8. What is the circumference of a circle with a radius of 10 cm?

9. For each image A, B, C and D, write whether it is a translation, reflection or rotation of the shaded L-shape:

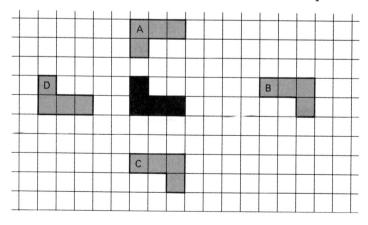

25

10. Find the value of:

    (*a*) 3^2 (*b*) 5^2 (*c*) 10^2 (*d*) 2^5

Mental Test 19 ======= Basic Algebra

1. To change yards into feet, multiply by 3. Change to feet:

    (*a*) 2 yd   (*b*) 6 yd   (*c*) 10 yd

2. The formula $A = lb$ gives the area of a rectangle. Find A when $l = 6$ and $b = 4$.

3. Find the value of:

    (*a*) $3 \times 4 + 5$ (*b*) $3 + 4 \times 5$

4. If $a = 7$ and $b = 6$, find the value of:

    (*a*) $a + b$ (*b*) ab (*c*) $ab + a$

5. Simplify:

    (*a*) $x + x + y + x + y + x + x + y + y$
    (*b*) $3m + 4n - m + 2n$

6. Sara had $5g$ pence. She spent $2g$ pence, then was given $6g$ pence. How much did she now have?

7. Simplify: (*a*) $3 \times 2k$ (*b*) $7 \times 4a$

8. If $c = 7$, $d = 2$ and $e = 5$, find the value of:

    (*a*) $c + d$ (*b*) $c - d - e$ (*c*) $cd - e$

Mental Test 20 ======= Statistics

1. The pictogram on the opposite page shows the number of packets of crisps sold at a school tuck shop.

Crisps Sold at a School Tuck Shop

Mon	🍟🍟🍟🍟🍟🍟🍟🍟🍟🍟🍟🍟🍟
Tues	🍟🍟🍟🍟🍟🍟🍟🍟🍟🍟🍟
Wed	🍟🍟🍟🍟🍟🍟🍟
Thurs	🍟🍟🍟🍟
Fri	🍟🍟🍟🍟🍟🍟🍟🍟🍟🍟🍟

Key: 🍟 represents 5 packets of crisps.

(a) How many packets of crisps were sold on Wednesday?
(b) On which day were the most packets of crisps sold?
(c) On which day were the fewest packets of crisps sold?
(d) How many packets of crisps were sold on Friday?

2. The bar chart below shows the pets owned by 2nd-year pupils.

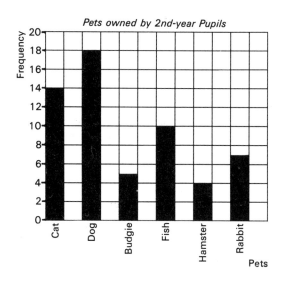

Pets owned by 2nd-year Pupils

(a) Which was the most popular pet?
(b) How many owned a cat?
(c) How many owned fish?
(d) Which was the least popular pet?

3. Here is a tally chart showing the goals scored in 45 football matches:

Number of goals	Tally	Frequency
0	~~||||~~ ~~||||~~ ~~||||~~ ~~||||~~ ~~||||~~		
1	~~||||~~ ~~||||~~ ~~||||~~ ~~||||~~ ~~||||~~ ~~||||~~ ~~||||~~	
2	~~||||~~ ~~||||~~ ~~||||~~ ||	
3	~~||||~~ |||	
4			
5					

(a) How many teams scored 2 goals?
(b) How many teams did not score?
(c) How many teams scored 1 goal?

4. The jagged line graph shows the average monthly temperature in Brussels:

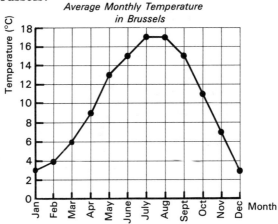

Average Monthly Temperature in Brussels

(a) What is the temperature in March?
(b) What is the temperature in November?
(c) In which month is the temperature 11 °C?
(d) In which two months is the temperature highest?
(e) In which two months is the temperature lowest?

5. In a pie chart, $360°$ stands for 20 people.
  (*a*) How many people does $180°$ stand for?
  (*b*) What angle is drawn to stand for 5 people?
  (*c*) What angle is drawn to stand for 1 person?

Mental Test 21 ━━━━━━━━━━━━━━ Simple Equations

1. What is the value of:
  (*a*) $12 - 12$?　　　(*b*) $29 + 13 - 13$?　(*c*) $61 - 19 + 19$?

2. Simplify: (*a*) $p + 8 - 8$　　　(*b*) $d - 14 + 14$

3. What is the missing number?
  (*a*) $x + 9 - \boxed{?} = x$　　　(*b*) $k - 10 + \boxed{?} = k$

4. For each question, find the missing number:
  (*a*) $\boxed{?} + 9 = 16$　　　(*b*) $\boxed{?} - 2 = 12$

5. (*a*) Does $m + 3 = 10$ when $m = 7$?
  (*b*) Does $n - 6 = 12$ when $n = 6$?
  (*c*) Does $l - 9 = 11$ when $l = 20$?
  (*d*) Does $h + 7 = 20$ when $h = 14$?

6. (*a*) Does $2d = 16$ when $d = 8$?
  (*b*) Does $5e = 45$ when $e = 9$?
  (*c*) Does $3n = 24$ when $n = 8$?
  (*d*) Does $4y = 36$ when $y = 8$?

7. Solve these equations:
  (*a*) $n + 8 = 14$　　　(*b*) $a - 8 = 11$

8. Solve these equations:
  (*a*) $2g = 18$　　　(*b*) $7u = 56$

1. Write the most suitable metric unit:
  (a) The width of a car is 1.65 ⟨ ? ⟩ .
  (b) The length of a pen is about 13 ⟨ ? ⟩ .

2. The length of a brick is about:
  A. 21 mm   B. 210 mm   C. 210 cm   D. 21 m

3. (a) How many metres are there in 4 km?
  (b) Change 20 mm into centimetres.
  (c) Change 9 m into centimetres.

4. A square has a perimeter of 36 cm. How long is each side?

5. Lynne is 5 ft tall. How many inches is that?

6. (a) Change 3 ℓ to millilitres. (c) Change 9.2 ℓ to millilitres.
  (b) Change 4000 mℓ to litres.

7. Given that 8 pt = 1 gal,
  (a) Change 5 gal to pints.
  (b) Change 32 pt to gallons.

8. A mug holds about:
  A. 100 mℓ   B. 250 mℓ   C. 1.2 ℓ   D. 200 ℓ

9. Ian has eight 500 mℓ cartons of milk.
  How many litres is that?

10. A new-born baby has a mass of about:
  A. 3 kg   B. 9 kg   C. 12 kg   D. 700 g

11. (a) Change 3 kg to grams.
  (b) Change 9.5 kg to grams.
  (c) Change 8000 g to kilograms.

12. (a) Change 8 g to milligrams.
  (b) Change 9000 mg to grams.

13. Given that 16 oz = 1 lb, how many ounces are there in 2 lb?

14. Which is heavier, 1 lb or 1 kg?

15. A golf ball has a mass of 50 g.
A cricket ball has a mass of 160 g.
Which is heavier, 3 golf balls or a cricket ball?

Mental Test 23 ━━━━━ Conversion Graphs and Tables

1. Use the conversion graph below to find the number of pints
in:
   (*a*) 10 gal   (*b*) 1 gal   (*c*) 6 gal   (*d*) 4 gal

2. Use the conversion graph below to find the number of gallons
in:
   (*a*) 40 pt   (*b*) 24 pt   (*c*) 64 pt   (*d*) 20 pt

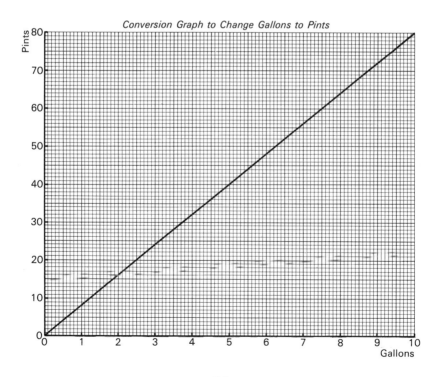

Conversion Graph to Change Gallons to Pints

31

3. The following conversion table can be used to change metres into feet or feet into metres:

Length

Metres	m or ft	Feet
0.30	1	3.28
0.61	2	6.56
0.91	3	9.84
1.22	4	13.13
1.52	5	16.41
1.83	6	19.69
2.13	7	22.97
2.44	8	26.25
2.74	9	29.53
3.05	10	32.82
6.10	20	65.63
9.14	30	98.45
12.19	40	131.27
15.24	50	164.08

Use the table to change:
(a) 3 m to feet
(b) 3 ft to metres
(c) 8 m to feet
(d) 10 m to feet
(e) 5 ft to metres
(f) 20 ft to metres
(g) 50 m to feet
(h) 9 m to feet
(i) 7 ft to metres

1. Vector $\overrightarrow{MN} = \begin{pmatrix} 3 \\ 1 \end{pmatrix}$. Write the vectors:

   (a) $\overrightarrow{PQ}$ (c) $\overrightarrow{QS}$ (e) $\overrightarrow{RU}$

   (b) $\overrightarrow{PT}$ (d) $\overrightarrow{RN}$ (f) $\overrightarrow{RT}$

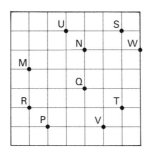

2. Which vector is $\begin{pmatrix} 5 \\ 2 \end{pmatrix}$?

3. Which vector is $\begin{pmatrix} 0 \\ 4 \end{pmatrix}$?

4. Which vector is $\begin{pmatrix} 1 \\ 1 \end{pmatrix}$?

5. Which vector is $\begin{pmatrix} 3 \\ 2 \end{pmatrix}$?

Mental Test 19 → 24 ═══════════════════════

1. $P = 6l$ gives the perimeter of a regular hexagon. Find P when $l = 8$.

2. Simplify $4 \times 6d$.

3. Simplify $5p + 2q - 2p + 7q - 3q$.

4. The tally chart shows the number of dresses sold each day at a certain shop:

Number of Dresses Sold at a Shop

Day	Tally	Frequency
Mon	﹀﹀﹀﹀﹀﹀ ||||	
Tues	﹀﹀﹀﹀﹀﹀ |||	
Wed	﹀﹀﹀﹀ ||	
Thurs	﹀﹀﹀﹀﹀﹀﹀﹀﹀﹀	
Fri	﹀﹀﹀﹀﹀﹀﹀﹀		
Sat	﹀﹀﹀﹀﹀﹀﹀﹀﹀﹀ |||	
Sun		

(a) How many dresses were sold on Tuesday?
(b) How many dresses were sold on Thursday?
(c) On which day were the most dresses sold?
(d) On which day were the fewest dresses sold (when at least one dress was sold)?
(e) On which day were no dresses sold?
(f) How many dresses were sold in the whole week?

5. The jagged line graph on the opposite page shows the rainfall in Nairobi.
   (a) In which month was there most rainfall?
   (b) In which month was there the least rainfall?
   (c) How much rainfall was there in March?
   (d) How much rainfall was there in September?
   (e) How much rainfall was there in May?
   (f) How much rainfall was there in December?

6. Find the value of:
   (a) 46 − 15 + 15   (b) 87 + 2 − 2

7. Does $x + 7 = 12$ when $x = 5$?

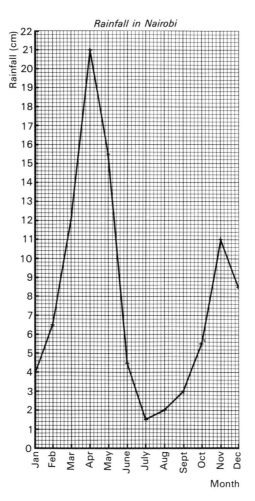

Rainfall in Nairobi

8. Does $4y = 36$ when $y = 9$?

9. Change 8000 m to kilometres.

10. A wine glass holds:
   A. 3.5 l B. 45 ml C. 350 ml D. 150 ml

11. A bike has a mass of 15 kg. A boy has a mass of 48 kg. How many kilograms is that altogether?

12. A pack of butter has a mass of 250 g.
   If I buy 8 packs, how many kilograms is that?

13. Use the conversion graph on p. 31 to change:

(*a*) 2 gal to pints   (*c*) 72 pt to gallons

(*b*) 7 gal to pints   (*d*) 60 pt to gallons

Conversion Tables

Length

Centimetres	cm or in	Inches
2.54	1	0.39
5.08	2	0.79
7.62	3	1.18
10.16	4	1.58
12.70	5	1.97
15.24	6	2.36
17.78	7	2.76
20.32	8	3.15
22.86	9	3.54
25.40	10	3.94
50.80	20	7.87
76.20	30	11.81
101.60	40	15.75
127.00	50	19.69

Mass

Kilograms	kg or lb	Pounds
0.45	1	2.20
0.91	2	4.41
1.36	3	6.61
1.81	4	8.82
2.27	5	11.02
2.72	6	13.23
3.18	7	15.43
3.63	8	17.64
4.08	9	19.84
4.54	10	22.05
9.07	20	44.09
13.61	30	66.14
18.14	40	88.18
22.68	50	110.2

Length

Kilometres	km or miles	Miles
1.61	1	0.62
3.22	2	1.24
4.83	3	1.86
6.44	4	2.49
8.05	5	3.11
9.66	6	3.73
11.27	7	4.35
12.87	8	4.97
14.48	9	5.59
16.09	10	6.21
32.19	20	12.43
48.28	30	18.64
64.37	40	24.85
80.47	50	31.07

Capacity

Litres	*l* or gal	Gallons
4.55	1	0.22
9.09	2	0.44
13.64	3	0.66
18.18	4	0.88
22.73	5	1.10
27.28	6	1.32
31.82	7	1.54
36.37	8	1.76
40.91	9	1.98
45.46	10	2.20
90.92	20	4.40
136.4	30	6.60
181.8	40	8.80
227.3	50	11.00

14. Use the conversion tables on p. 36 to change:

(a) 4 cm to inches   (e) 30 ℓ to gallons

(b) 10 km to miles   (f) 40 kg to pounds

(c) 6 lb to kilograms   (g) 5 miles to km

(d) 20 in to centimetres   (h) 2 gal to litres

15. Write the vector:

(a) $\overrightarrow{XY}$ (e) $\overrightarrow{ZX}$

(b) $\overrightarrow{ZV}$ (f) $\overrightarrow{ZY}$

(c) $\overrightarrow{WY}$ (g) $\overrightarrow{WX}$

(d) $\overrightarrow{VY}$ (h) $\overrightarrow{ZW}$

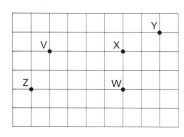

Mental Test 13 → 24

1. Write these numbers in order of size. Put the smallest first.

(a) $^-12, \, ^+4, \, ^-2$ (b) $^-3, \, ^-16, \, ^-1, 0$

2. Use the number line on p. 18 to help with these:

(a) $^-2 + 5$ (b) $7 - 9$ (c) $^-4 - 5$ (d) $^-9 + 3$

3. Answer these using the given relation:

(a) What does 2 map to?

(b) What does 6 map to?

(c) What maps to 20?

(d) What maps to 28?

(e) What does 0 map to?

(f) What maps to 12?

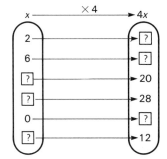

4. Use the shapes drawn on p. 25 to answer these:

(a) Which side of the trapezium is parallel to AB?

(b) Give the co-ordinates of the vertices of the isosceles triangle.

(c) The point $(^-2, 6)$ is a vertex of a certain quadrilateral. What sort of quadrilateral is it?

(d) Give the co-ordinates of the point where the diagonals of the rhombus intersect.

5. What is the circumference of a circle with a radius of 4 cm?

6. For each image A, B, C, D and E, write whether it is a translation, a reflection or a rotation of the black shaded L-shape shown.

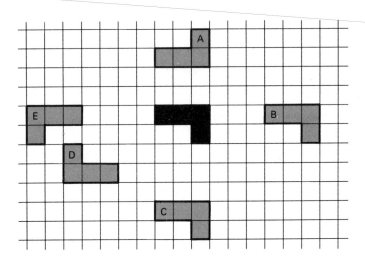

7. Find the value of:
(*a*) 3^2 (*b*) 8^2 (*c*) 11^2 (*d*) 2^4

8. $C = \pi d$ gives the circumference of a circle.
Find C when $\pi = 3$ and $d = 7$.

9. Simplify $3m + 5n + m - 2n - 2m$.

10. The pictogram on the opposite page shows how Nikki spent the day. Use the graph to help with these:
(*a*) How long did Nikki watch TV?
(*b*) How long did Nikki work?
(*c*) How long did Nikki spend eating?
(*d*) How long did Nikki spend sleeping?

11. Does $m - 6 = 9$ when $m = 15$?

12. Does $5n = 35$ when $n = 9$?

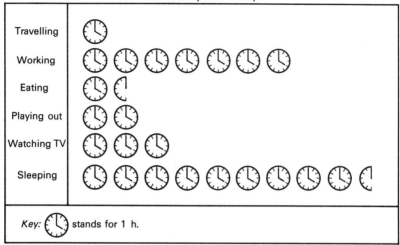

13. Change 9 m to millimetres.

14. How many 250 m*l* mugs can be filled from 2 *l* of water?

15. Use the conversion tables on p. 36 to change:
- (*a*) 2 kg to pounds
- (*b*) 5 gal to litres
- (*c*) 30 cm to inches
- (*d*) 40 miles to kilometres

16. Write the vectors:
- (*a*) $\overrightarrow{AC}$
- (*d*) $\overrightarrow{EB}$
- (*b*) $\overrightarrow{AB}$
- (*e*) $\overrightarrow{ED}$
- (*c*) $\overrightarrow{AD}$
- (*f*) $\overrightarrow{CB}$

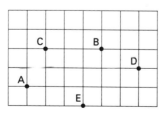

1. How many members has the set of whole numbers that lie between 30 and 40?

2. How many members has {months of the year}?

3. 4 × 7000.

4. A watch costs £6.95. How much change should you get out of £10?

5. Here are two quadrilaterals:

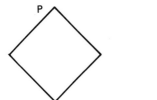 

   (a) Write the names of the quadrilaterals.
   (b) Write P if only shape P has bilateral symmetry.
       Write Q if only shape Q has bilateral symmetry.
       Write PQ if both shapes have bilateral symmetry.
   (c) Write P if only shape P has rotational symmetry.
       Write Q if only shape Q has rotational symmetry.
       Write PQ if both shapes have rotational symmetry.

6. How many fifths are there in $4\frac{2}{5}$?

7. Calculate the missing angles (labelled θ):
   (a)   (b)

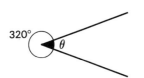

8. Write 8.6 correct to the nearest whole number.

9. Write $5\frac{9}{10}$ as a decimal.

10. How many times bigger is the first quantity than the second?
(a) £16, £4   (b) 2 min, 30 s   (c) 1 cm, 2 mm

11. Using a scale of 1 cm to 8 km, what would be the true length of a line that is:
(a) 2 cm long?   (b) 4 cm long?   (c) 3 cm long?

12. Christmas cards are sold in boxes of eight. How many cards would there be if there were:
(a) 2 boxes and 2 cards left over?
(b) 4 boxes and 3 cards left over?

13. How many minutes are there in $1\frac{1}{4}$ h?

14. Which is the fifth month of the year?

15. Calculate the area of a parallelogram with base 9 cm and perpendicular height 4 cm.

16. Find 50% of £32.

17. Which is warmer, $^{-}9\,°C$ or $^{-}4\,°C$?

18. Answer these using the given mapping diagram:
(a) What does 3 map to?
(b) What does 7 map to?
(c) What does $^{-}4$ map to?
(d) What maps to 10?
(e) What maps to 5?
(f) What maps to 0?

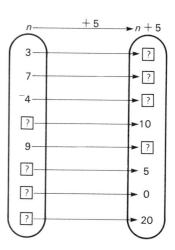

19. Use the shapes drawn on p. 25 to answer these:
    (*a*) What are the co-ordinates of the centre of the circle?
    (*b*) The point ($^{-}$2, 8) is a vertex of a certain shape. What is the name of that shape?

20. Find the circumference of a circle with a diameter of 12 cm.

21. For each image A, B and C, write whether it is a translation, reflection or rotation of the shaded black L-shape:

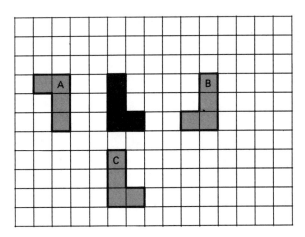

22. Find the value of:
    (*a*) 7^2 (*b*) 5^2 (*c*) 12^2 (*d*) 2^3

23. To change metres into centimetres, multiply by 100. Change to centimetres:
    (*a*) 6 m   (*b*) 14 m   (*c*) 35 m

24. The bar chart on the opposite page shows the attendance at a cinema during a certain week:
    (*a*) How many were at the cinema on Monday?
    (*b*) How many were at the cinema on Sunday?
    (*c*) How many were at the cinema on Thursday?
    (*d*) On which day were 250 people at the cinema?
    (*e*) Which was the most popular day?

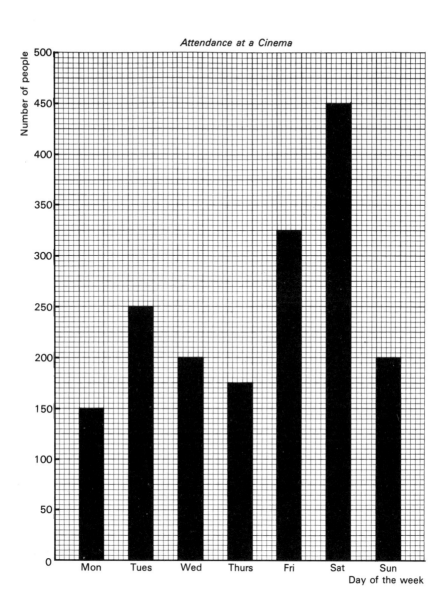

Attendance at a Cinema

25. Does $p - 8 = 8$ when $p = 0$?

26. Does $7q = 56$ when $q = 8$?

27. (a) Change 8 cm to millimetres.

(b) Change 6000 mm to metres.

(c) Change 6 ℓ to millilitres.

(d) Change 9000 mℓ to litres.

(e) Change 2000 g to kilograms.

(f) Change 12 g to milligrams.

28. Use the conversion tables on p. 36 to change:

(a) 8 ℓ to gallons   (c) 40 lb to kilograms

(b) 3 in to centimetres   (d) 20 km to miles

29. Vector $\overrightarrow{KN} = \begin{pmatrix} 1 \\ 4 \end{pmatrix}$. Write the vectors:

(a) $\overrightarrow{JK}$ (c) $\overrightarrow{NP}$

(b) $\overrightarrow{KM}$ (d) $\overrightarrow{MP}$

30. Which vector is:

(a) $\begin{pmatrix} 2 \\ 1 \end{pmatrix}$?   (c) $\begin{pmatrix} 1 \\ 1 \end{pmatrix}$?

(b) $\begin{pmatrix} 3 \\ 2 \end{pmatrix}$?   (d) $\begin{pmatrix} 0 \\ 3 \end{pmatrix}$?

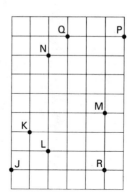

Phase Tests

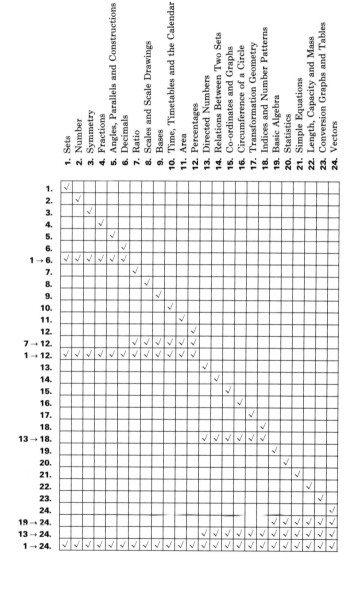

	1. Sets	2. Number	3. Symmetry	4. Fractions	5. Angles, Parallels and Constructions	6. Decimals	7. Ratio	8. Scales and Scale Drawings	9. Bases	10. Time, Timetables and the Calendar	11. Area	12. Percentages	13. Directed Numbers	14. Relations Between Two Sets	15. Co-ordinates and Graphs	16. Circumference of a Circle	17. Transformation Geometry	18. Indices and Number Patterns	19. Basic Algebra	20. Statistics	21. Simple Equations	22. Length, Capacity and Mass	23. Conversion Graphs and Tables	24. Vectors
1.	✓																							
2.		✓																						
3.			✓																					
4.				✓																				
5.					✓																			
6.						✓																		
1 → 6.	✓	✓	✓	✓	✓	✓																		
7.							✓																	
8.								✓																
9.									✓															
10.										✓														
11.											✓													
12.												✓												
7 → 12.							✓	✓	✓	✓	✓	✓												
1 → 12.	✓	✓	✓	✓	✓	✓	✓	✓	✓	✓	✓	✓												
13.													✓											
14.														✓										
15.															✓									
16.																✓								
17.																	✓							
18.																		✓						
13 → 18.													✓	✓	✓	✓	✓	✓						
19.																			✓					
20.																				✓				
21.																					✓			
22.																						✓		
23.																							✓	
24.																								✓
19 → 24.																			✓	✓	✓	✓	✓	✓
13 → 24.													✓	✓	✓	✓	✓	✓	✓	✓	✓	✓	✓	✓
1 → 24.	✓	✓	✓	✓	✓	✓	✓	✓	✓	✓	✓	✓	✓	✓	✓	✓	✓	✓	✓	✓	✓	✓	✓	✓

1. Which of these are simple closed curves?

(a) 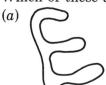 (b)  (c)

2. (a) Draw a simple closed curve.
(b) Draw a curve that is not a simple closed curve.

3. Show on a Venn diagram, the set of numbers less than 20 that divide exactly by 3.

4. List, using curly brackets, the set of letters of the alphabet between m and t.

5. Which is the wrong member in the set?
a set of trees = {ash, beach, elm, pine, oak}.

6. Find the missing members in the set of numbers between 120 and 200 that have a units digit of 4:
{124, ? , 144, 154, 164, ? , ? , 194}.

7. Here is a set of numbers: {7, 15, 23, 29, 36, 48}. Write the set of numbers in which each member is three times as big as the members of the set above.

8. Copy these. Replace each box with $\in$ or $\notin$ to make each sentence true.
(a) 39 ? {odd numbers}
(b) 60 ? {factors of 30}
(c) rhombus ? {triangles}

9. kite $\notin$ {quadrilaterals}
Write A if the statement above is true. Write B if it is false.

10. Is the set of multiples of 8 with a units digit of 5 an empty set?

11. How many members has the set of factors of 15?

12. Draw a diagram such as the one given, where a circle, square and triangle overlap.
Fill in the missing numbers so that the circle total = 36, the square total = 34, and the triangle total = 41.

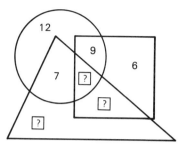

Phase Test 2

1. Write these numbers in order. Put the smallest first.
623, 509, 396, 1904, 2993, 1009, 716, 1344

2. Using the digits 4, 5 and 8, make as many 2-digit numbers as you can.

3. Copy and complete this mapping diagram:

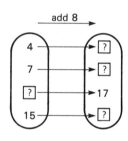

4. 2 + 4 + 6 + 8 = 20. Find the value of 12 + 14 + 16 + 18.

5. Copy this but put the missing sign + or − in place of each box:

$$8 \boxed{?} 2 \boxed{?} 9 = 15$$

6. Answer these:

(a) 4692
  + 1657

(b) 7603
  − 2466

7. There are 24 stamps on each page. How many stamps are there on 6 pages?

8. Copy and complete this mapping diagram:

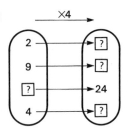

9. 700 × 40.

10. 57 × 300.

11. Estimate 49 × 31.

12. In the calculation 63 × 21 as shown, some digits have been missed out.
Copy and complete the calculation.

```
          6 3
    ×     2 1
   ?  ?  6 0    20 × 63
   +      ? 3    1 × 63
    ?  3  ?  ?
```

13. If a box of matches holds 53 matches, how many matches will 7 boxes hold?

14. Does 16 × 34 = 8 × 68?

15. Groceries cost £14.68. How much change did I get out of £20?

16. How much per year is £73 per month?

17. Copy this, but write a number in place of the box to make the calculation correct:

$$14 + \boxed{?} = 6 \times 4$$

18. Copy the following. Put in the missing sign $>$, $<$ or $=$

$$120 \div 4 \boxed{?} 92 - 63$$

19. Here is a set of numbers: $\{27, 35, 36, 59, 90, 117, 123\}$.
(a) Which of the numbers are odd?
(b) Which of the numbers divide exactly by 9?

20. Write a number less than 100 that divides exactly by 9 and by 10.

Phase Test 3 ══════════════════════════ Symmetry

1. Copy the following. Complete each letter so that the broken lines are axes of symmetry.

2. Draw a rectangle. Mark on it its axes of symmetry.

3. Copy the given shape on to squared paper. Complete it so that the broken lines are axes of symmetry.

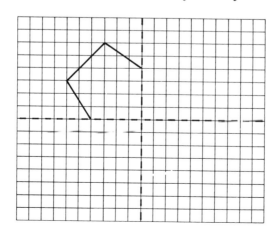

4. Which of these shapes have rotational symmetry?

(a)   (b)   (c)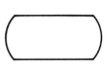

Phase Test 4 ================================== Fractions

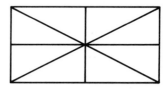

1. Copy the shape and shade $\frac{5}{8}$.

2. On another copy of the shape, shade $\frac{3}{4}$.

3. Dan had 90 p. He spent 60 p. What fraction did he spend?

4. Write in words, $\frac{7}{12}$.

5. Copy and complete: $\dfrac{15}{18} = \dfrac{\boxed{?}}{6}$.

6. Copy and complete the set of equivalent fractions:

$$\frac{3}{5} = \frac{\boxed{?}}{10} = \frac{9}{\boxed{?}} = \frac{12}{\boxed{?}} = \frac{\boxed{?}}{25} = \frac{\boxed{?}}{30} = \frac{\boxed{?}}{50} = \frac{\boxed{?}}{100}$$

7. Simplify $\frac{12}{16}$.

8. Which is bigger:
(a) $\frac{5}{8}$ or $\frac{7}{8}$? (b) $\frac{3}{4}$ or $\frac{3}{8}$?

9. Which is bigger, $\frac{3}{5}$ or $\frac{7}{10}$?

10. Put these fractions in order of size, largest first: $\frac{1}{2}, \frac{3}{4}, \frac{7}{12}$.

11. (a) Write $1\frac{4}{5}$ as an improper fraction.
(b) Write $\frac{14}{3}$ as a mixed number.

12. Write 20 fifths as a whole number.

13. Jenny was laying carpet tiles in her kitchen. She had 36 tiles to lay. After laying $\frac{3}{4}$ of them, how many tiles were left?

14. Copy the crosses. On your copy, ring $\frac{2}{5}$ of the crosses. (Use a simple closed curve.)

15. Find $\frac{7}{10}$ of £1 in pence.

16. Find $\frac{3}{4}$ of £28.

17. Carry out these calculations:

(a) $\dfrac{4}{9} + \dfrac{3}{9}$ 　　　　　　　(b) $\dfrac{9}{16} - \dfrac{2}{16}$

18. Carry out these calculations. Simplify your answers.

(a) $\dfrac{9}{16} + \dfrac{1}{16}$ 　　　　　　(b) $\dfrac{7}{10} - \dfrac{3}{10}$

19. Carry out the calculation $1 - \dfrac{3}{10}$.

20. Carry out the multiplication $3 \times \dfrac{5}{8}$.

Phase Test 5 ━━━━━ Angles, Parallels and Constructions

1. Write whether each angle is an acute angle, an obtuse angle, a reflex angle or a right-angle:

(a) 　　　　　　 (b) 　　　　　　　 (c)

2. Measure these angles:

(a)

(b)

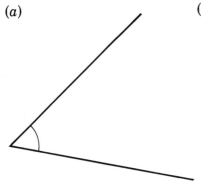

3. How many degrees are there in:

(a) $\frac{1}{3}$ turn?   (b) $\frac{1}{8}$ turn?   (c) $\frac{1}{6}$ turn?   (d) $\frac{5}{8}$ turn?

4. Calculate the missing angles (labelled θ):

(a)

(b)

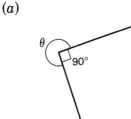
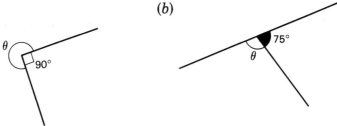

5. (a) Measure $\angle$ LMP.
   (b) Measure $\angle$ PMN.

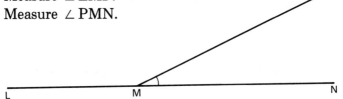

6. (a) Draw any parallelogram. Label it ABCD.
   (b) Draw diagonal BD.
   (c) Mark on your drawing $\angle$ BDC.
   (d) Which side is parallel to DA?

7. Construct a hexagon with sides 25 mm.

8. Draw a straight line 65 mm long.
Bisect the line using a pair of compasses.

9. Draw an angle of 65° using a protractor.
Bisect the angle with a pair of compasses.

10. Construct △WXY where XY = 64 mm, WY = 40 mm
and WX = 50 mm.

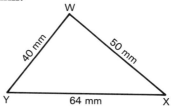

Using a pair of compasses, bisect WY. Let the bisector cut
XY at Z.
Measure YZ.

Phase Test 6 — Decimals

1. In the number 348.72 what is the value of the underlined
digit?

2. Change these common fractions to decimals:

(a) $\dfrac{2}{10}$ (b) $\dfrac{78}{100}$ (c) $6\dfrac{3}{10}$ (d) $2\dfrac{37}{100}$ (e) $\dfrac{1}{2}$

3. Answer these:
(a) 46.5 + 27.8 (b) 54.63 − 21.72

4. Answer these:
(a) 4.9 + 28 + 16.58 (b) 80.47 − 36.74

5. Write 74.8 correct to the nearest whole number.

6. Write these numbers correct to 1 significant figure:
(a) 6.17 (b) 86.34 (c) 44.99 (d) 751.2

7. Estimate the answers to these. Work with 1 significant figure.

(*a*) 89.31 × 4

(*b*) 62.95 ÷ 3

8. Work out these:

(*a*) 29.03 × 5

(*b*) 29.52 ÷ 6

9. Each side of a square measures 5.8 cm. Calculate its perimeter.

10. A piece of wood is 2.32 m long. It is cut into four equal lengths. How long is each length?

11. Laura's bus fare was £1.78 per day. How much did 5 days' bus fare cost?

12. Copy and complete the invoice:

			£ p
6	cups	@ £2.55	15.30
6	saucers	@ £1.70	
8	small plates	@ £2.10	
6	medium plates	@ £3.25	
6	large plates	@ £4.45	
8	dishes	@ £2.90	
		Total cost	

Phase Test 1 → 6

1. Show on a Venn diagram the set of numbers between 18 and 58 that divide exactly by 5.

2. Using curly brackets and commas, list the set of prime numbers that lie between 6 and 25.

3. Is it true that $32 \in \{\text{multiples of } 4\}$?

4. Write 39 in words.

5. Janine spent £3.56 in a shop. How much change did she get out of £5?

6. There are 28 sweets in a box. How many sweets are there in 4 boxes?

7. Copy and complete the mapping:

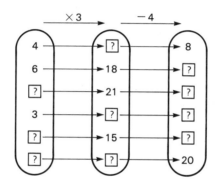

8. Copy the word NAMES for both parts of the question. Reflect it in the given axis of symmetry. Draw the reflection.

(*a*)   (*b*)

9. Name a triangle that has rotational symmetry.

10. Which is bigger,
   (*a*) $\frac{7}{10}$ or $\frac{7}{8}$?   (*b*) $\frac{2}{3}$ or $\frac{7}{12}$?

11. Maria had £15. She spent $\frac{2}{3}$ of it.
   (*a*) How much did she spend?
   (*b*) How much did she have left?

12. Measure these angles:

(a)

(b)

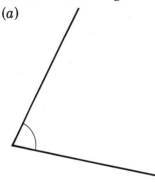

13. Construct an equilateral triangle with sides of length 50 mm.

14. Each side of a regular hexagon measures 43 mm. Find its perimeter.

15. Ron set off shopping with £20. He spent £6.45 in one shop and £5.80 in another.
How much money did he have left?

Phase Test 7 ════════════════════════════ Ratio

1. ─────────────────

Draw a straight line that is four times as long as the line above.

2. Draw a rectangle where each side is half the length of each side of the rectangle shown.

3. How many times as big as 9 cm is 36 cm?

4. How many times as big as 15 min is 2 h?

5. Draw a straight line $\frac{1}{4}$ the length of the given line:

_____

6. What fraction of £6 is £1.50?

7. What fraction of 30 m is 20 m?

8. The ingredients for mustard steaks for four people are given. Copy the ingredients but give the quantities for two people.

Mustard steaks
  4   fillet steaks (800 g)
         salt and pepper
 50 g   butter
142 m*l* double cream
 10 m*l* French mustard

Phase Test 8 ═══════════════ Scales and Scale Drawings

1. The line below has been drawn to a scale of 1 cm to 4 km. Find its true length.

_____

2. The drawing shows a room. It has been drawn to a scale of 1 cm to 2 m.
  (*a*) How long is the room?
  (*b*) What is the width of the room?
  (*c*) How far is it from one corner to the opposite corner?

3. Use a scale of 1 cm to 1 m to draw a line 5 m long.

4. Use a scale of 1 cm to 1 m to draw a line 8 m long.

5. A ship sails 8 km due west from P. It then turns North and sails 6 km to Q.
Make a scale drawing of the journey.
Use a scale of 1 cm to 1 km.
Use your drawing to find the direct distance from P to Q.

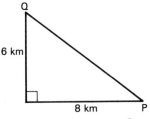

Phase Test 9 ═══════════════════ Bases

1. (a) Copy the crosses.
   (b) Draw around groups of eight.
   (c) How many groups of eight are there?
   (d) How many crosses are left over?

2. (a) Copy the crosses.
   (b) Draw around groups of five.
   (c) How many groups of five are there?
   (d) How many crosses are left over?

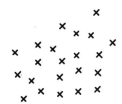

3. $25_6 = \boxed{?}$ sixes $+ \boxed{?}$ units $= \boxed{?} + \boxed{?} = \boxed{?}_{\text{ten}}$
Copy and complete.

4. Light bulbs are in packs of five. How many bulbs are there altogether if there are:
   (a) 2 packs?
   (b) 2 packs and 4 extra bulbs?
   (c) 4 packs and 2 extra bulbs?

5. (a) Write 12_8 in base ten.
   (b) Write 56_8 in base ten.

1. How many days are there in 4 weeks?

2. How many minutes are there in $2\frac{1}{2}$ hours?

3. Write 190 min in hours and minutes.

4. Write 21.30 using the 12-hour clock.

5. Write 11.00 a.m. using the 24-hour clock.

6. What time is shown on the given clock if it is evening?
   (*a*) Give the time using the 12-hour clock.
   (*b*) Give the time using the 24-hour clock.

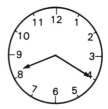

7. Write ten past seven in the morning in figures using the 24-hour clock.

8. 15.25 is twenty-five past three in the afternoon, so:
   (*a*) Write 18.05 in words,
   (*b*) Write 04.50 in words.

9. It is now 14.55. How many minutes are there to 15.30?

10. Sharon caught the bus at 20.25. Her bus journey took 30 min. At what time did she get off the bus?

11. Which is the sixth month of the year?

12. How many days are there in November?

13. If 14 April was a Sunday, what day was 25 April?

59

14. Answer these using the timetable given:
  (a) If you leave Bristol Parkway at 13.40, at what time would you arrive in Plymouth?
  (b) If you leave Exeter at 18.07, at what time would you arrive in Taunton?
  (c) A train arrived at Bristol Parkway at 14.16. At what time did it leave Exeter?
  (d) A train arrived in Plymouth at 19.56. At what time did it leave Taunton?

Bristol Parkway → Plymouth

Bristol Parkway	09.43	13.40	17.28	19.33
Taunton	10.37	14.34	18.26	20.25
Exeter	11.04	15.03	18.55	20.54
Plymouth	12.17	16.08	19.56	22.00

Plymouth → Bristol Parkway

Plymouth	07.05	11.38	14.05	17.00
Exeter	08.03	12.42	15.06	18.07
Taunton	08.31	13.13	15.32	18.33
Bristol Parkway	09.22	14.16	16.25	19.28

15. 17 October 1963 can be written as 17.10.63.
  (a) Write 21 March 1974 in figures.
  (b) Write 30.6.82 using the name of the month.

1. How many small squares are there in the rectangle shown?

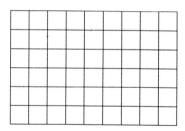

2. Calculate the area of a rectangle of length 6 cm and breadth 7 cm.

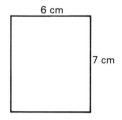

3. Calculate the area of a rectangle of length 8.2 m and breadth 4 m.

4. Calculate the shaded area:

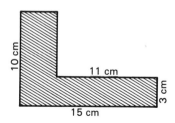

5. Calculate the missing length of a rectangle of area 105 m² if its breadth is 7 m.

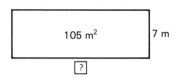

6. Draw a net of a cuboid that is 6 cm by 5 cm by 3 cm. Calculate its surface area.

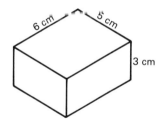

7. Calculate the area of the parallelogram shown.

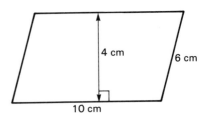

8. Calculate the area of a parallelogram with base 9 cm and perpendicular height 3.4 cm.

9. Calculate the area of the triangle shown.

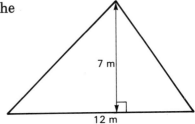

10. Calculate the area of a triangle with base 28 cm and perpendicular height 13 cm.

Phase Test 12 ══════════════════ Percentages

1. What percentage of the big square has been shaded?

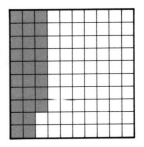

2. Draw a square with sides of 40 mm length. Shade 25% of it.

3. Write as percentages:
(a) 67 out of 100   (b) $\frac{36}{100}$ (c) $\frac{97}{100}$

4. Write each percentage as a common fraction:

    (*a*) 43%   (*b*) 81%   (*c*) 75%

5. Change to decimals:

    (*a*) 38%   (*b*) 95%   (*c*) 12%

6. (*a*) Find 50% of £9.   (*c*) Find 75% of £16.

    (*b*) Find 25% of £28.

Phase Test 7 → 12

1. Enlarge the given rectangle.
Make each side 3 times as long.

2. Colin walked 21 km. Ann walked $\frac{2}{3}$ of that distance.
How far did Ann walk?

3. ABCD is a trapezium.
It has been drawn to a
scale of 1 cm to 2 m.

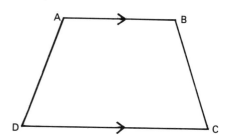

    (*a*) Find the true length of side BC.
    (*b*) Find the true length of the side that is parallel to side AB.
    (*c*) Find the true length of diagonal BD.

4. Use a scale of 1 cm to 5 km to draw these lines:

    (*a*) 30 km   (*h*) 25 km

5. Ballpoint pens are sold in packs of eight. How many ballpoint
pens are there in:

    (*a*) 2 packs and 4 pens left over?
    (*b*) 6 packs and 3 pens left over?

6. 18 March 1985 can be written 18.3.85.
Write 24 October 1986 in figures.

7. Answer these using the timetable given:
  (a) If you leave Sheffield at 16.48, at what time would you
      arrive in Birmingham?
  (b) If you leave Derby at 13.04, at what time would you arrive
      in York?

Newcastle → Birmingham

Newcastle	08.10	09.08	12.37	14.37	16.06
York	09.26	10.18	13.46	15.46	17.43
Sheffield	10.48	11.18	14.48	16.48	18.49
Derby	11.27	12.00	15.27	17.27	19.40
Birmingham	12.15	12.48	16.15	18.15	20.34

Birmingham → Newcastle

Birmingham	07.45	09.45	12.12	16.45	17.45
Derby	08.38	10.33	13.04	17.35	18.33
Sheffield	09.20	11.12	13.53	18.17	19.12
York	10.22	12.14	14.58	19.44	20.14
Newcastle	11.32	13.20	16.43	21.10	21.25

  (c) Find when you must leave Birmingham to arrive in
      Newcastle at 21.10.
  (d) At what time must you leave York to arrive in Sheffield
      at 11.18?

8. Calculate the area of the shaded shape:

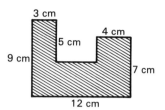

9. Calculate the area of a parallelogram with base 8.4 cm and perpendicular height 6 cm.

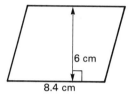

10. Change to common fractions:
(*a*) 63%　　　　　(*b*) 99%　　　　　(*c*) 25%

11. Change to decimals:
(*a*) 63%　　　　　(*b*) 87%　　　　　(*c*) 5%

12. (*a*) Find 50% of £80.
(*b*) Find 25% of £60.
(*c*) Find 75% of £10.

Phase Test 1 → 12

1. Here is a set of numbers: {10, 12, 15, 19, 35, 43}. Write the set of numbers in which each member is twice as big as the members of the set above.

2. List the set of factors of 28. Use curly brackets and commas.

3. Find the value of 3×264.

4. Which of these numbers divide exactly by 9?
{14, 18, 25, 34, 45, 57, 69, 72, 84, 90, 108, 144, 158}

5. Copy the given shape on to squared paper. Complete it so that the broken line is an axis of symmetry.

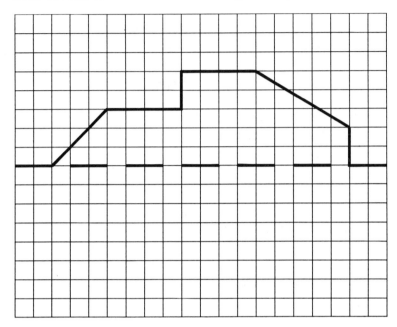

6. Tim had 84 p. If he spent $\frac{1}{4}$ of his money, how much would be left?

7. Find $\dfrac{9}{10} - \dfrac{3}{10}$.

8. (a) Carefully copy the diagram shown.
   (b) Join and measure AB.

9. Calculate the missing angles (labelled θ):

(a)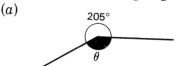

(b)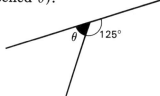

10. Find the value of:

(a) $83.27 + 19.91$ (b) 7.68×3

11. Maria lives 8 km away from school. Gary lives at $\frac{3}{4}$ of that distance away. How far from school does Gary live?

12. ─────────

Draw a straight line that is 5 times the length of the line above.

13. Parallelogram ABCD has been drawn to a scale of 1 cm to 4 cm.

(a) What is the true length of AB?

(b) What is the true length of the side that is parallel to DA?

(c) What is the true length of the longest diagonal?

14. Crayons are sold in packs of eight. How many crayons are there in:

(a) 1 pack with 2 crayons left over?

(b) 4 packs with 6 crayons left over?

15. Answer these using the timetable on p. 64.

(a) If you leave Newcastle at 16.06, at what time would you arrive in Derby?

(b) If you leave Sheffield at 09.20, at what time would you arrive in Newcastle?

(c) Find when you must leave York to arrive in Birmingham at 16.15.

(d) How long does the journey take to Birmingham on the train that leaves York at 10.18?

16. Calculate the area of the triangle shown.

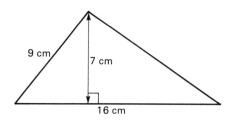

17. Change to decimals:
(a) 28% (b) 54% (c) 20%

18. Find 25% of £52.

Phase Test 13  Directed Numbers

1. Which is warmer, ⁻12 °C or ⁻7 °C?

2. Write these temperatures in order, from coldest to hottest:
16 °C, ⁻4 °C, 0 °C, ⁻10 °C, ⁻16 °C, 8 °C, ⁻2 °C.

3. Here is a list of temperatures:
⁻7 °C, 4 °C, 9 °C, ⁻8 °C, 3 °C, ⁻5 °C, ⁻12 °C, ⁻13 °C
(a) Which is the lowest temperature in the list?
(b) Which is the fourth highest temperature in the list?
(c) Which are the temperatures that are colder than ⁻5 °C?

4. Copy the following number line and fill in the missing numbers:

⁻18   0   ⁺6

5. Write whether each of the following is true or false:
(a) ⁻3 < ⁻9 (b) ⁻16 < ⁻8 (c) ⁻1 > ⁻5

6. Copy the following but use $>$ or $<$ in place of each box to make the statement correct:
    (a) $^-10$ [?] $^-2$
    (b) $^+2$ [?] $^-6$
    (c) $^-4$ [?] $^-5$

7. Write $^-5, 0, ^-2, ^+9, ^-8$ in order of size. Put the biggest first.

8. Mrs Barker had £60 in her bank account. How much would she have to spend to leave an overdraft of £20?

9. Use the number line to help with these:
    (a) $^-13 + 11$
    (b) $^-8 - 6$
    (c) $^+7 - 12$
    (d) $^-5 + 14$

10. The temperature is $^-4\,°C$. If it rises by $5\,°C$ what is the new temperature?

11. Use the number line to help with these. Remember, $4\uparrow$ means a journey 4 places upwards and $3\downarrow$ means a journey 3 places downwards.
    (a) $5\uparrow + 9\downarrow$
    (b) $3\downarrow + 8\downarrow$
    (c) $2\downarrow + 7\uparrow$

12. Use the number line to help with these:
    (a) $6\uparrow + 10\downarrow$
    (b) $12\uparrow + 12\downarrow$
    (c) $17\downarrow + 17\uparrow$

1. Copy and complete the mapping diagram to show the number of axes of bilateral symmetry for the shapes given.

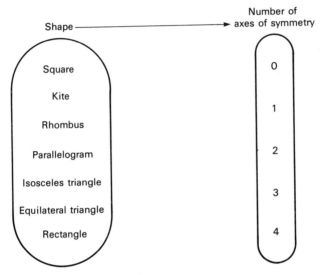

2. Copy and complete the given mapping diagram.

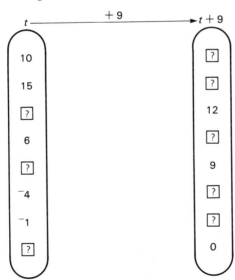

3. If $y = 5$, find the value of:
   (a) $y + 9$ (b) $y - 9$ (c) $2y$ (d) $3y + 2$

1. Draw a pair of axes as shown.

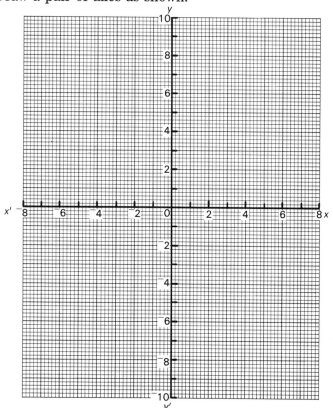

Use a scale of 1 cm to 1 unit on both axes. Label the x-axis from ⁻8 to ⁺8. Label the y-axis from ⁻10 to ⁺10.

Answer the following on the same piece of graph paper, using the same pair of axes:

(a) Plot the points A(2, 8) and B(6, 6). Join AB. What are the co-ordinates of the mid-point of AB?

(b) Plot the points C(⁻5, ⁻4), D(⁻5, ⁻7) and E(1, ⁻7), and join them in that order with straight lines.
Find and plot a point F such that CDEF is a rectangle. Complete the rectangle.
What are the co-ordinates of F?

(c) Plot the points G(⁻4, 8), H(⁻4, 5), I(2, 3) and J(2, 6), and join them in that order using straight lines.
Complete the quadrilateral. What sort of quadrilateral is it?

(d) $(^-3, 3)$, $(^-5, 0)$ and $(^-2, ^-2)$ are three vertices of a square. Plot them and draw the square.
What are the co-ordinates of the fourth vertex?

2.

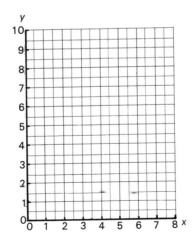

is 4 less than			x	y
x → **y**				
6	10	(6, 10)	6	10
5	?	(5, ?)	5	?
4	?	(4, ?)	4	?
3	?	(3, ?)	3	?
2	?	(2, ?)	2	?
1	?	(1, ?)	1	?
0	?	(0, ?)	0	?

(a) Copy and complete the mapping diagram for the relation 'is 4 less than'.
(b) Copy and complete the pairs of co-ordinates.
(c) Copy and complete the table.
(d) Draw a pair of axes as shown. Use a scale of 2 cm to 1 unit on both axes.

(e) Graph the relation 'is 4 less than'.

72

3. Books cost £6 each. The table below shows the cost of buying up to 8 books.

Number of books, n	0	1	2	3	4	5	6	7	8
Cost of books, C (£)	0	6		18					48

(a) Copy and complete the table.
(b) Draw a pair of axes as shown. Use a scale of 2 cm to 1 book on the horizontal axis and 2 cm to £5 (1 cm to £2.50) on the vertical axis.
(c) Use the table to help you to draw a graph.

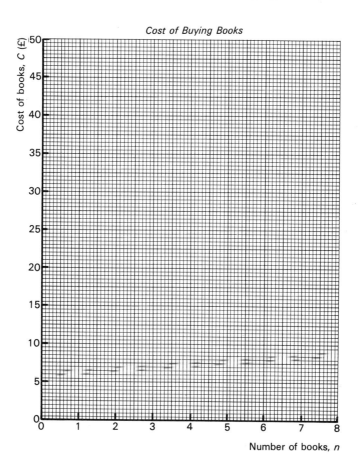

Cost of Buying Books

Phase Test 16 ━━━━━━━ Circumference of a Circle

Throughout this test, use:
Circumference of circle = 3 × diameter.

1. What is the radius of a circle with a diameter of 34 mm?

2. What is the circumference of a circle with a diameter of 23 cm?

3. What is the circumference of a circle with a radius of 16 cm?

4. Find the circumference of a circle with a diameter of 8.5 cm.

5. A jam jar has a diameter of 58 mm.
   (a) What is the circumference of the jar?
   (b) If a label goes half-way around the jar, how long is the label?

Phase Test 17 ━━━━━━━ Transformation Geometry

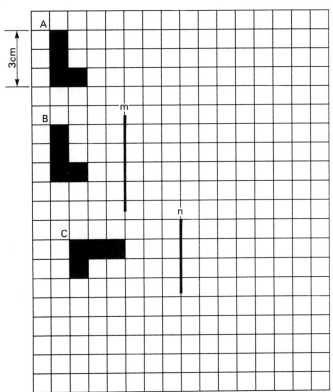

1. Copy L-shape A and translate it 5 cm to the right. Draw the image.

2. Copy L-shape B and mirror line m. Reflect B in the mirror line. Draw the image.

3. Copy L-shape C and mirror line n. Reflect C in the mirror line. Draw the image.

4. If the given shape is rotated through $\frac{1}{4}$ turn clockwise, draw the image position.

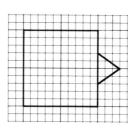

Phase Test 18 ——————— Indices and Number Patterns

1. Write in index form: $p \times p \times p \times p \times p \times p \times p \times p$.

2. Find the value of:
   (a) 1^2 (b) 8^2 (c) 5^3 (d) 4^3

3. Find the value of t^6 when $t = 2$.

4. Use a calculator to find the value of:
   (a) 2.9^2 (b) 31.6^2 (c) 0.41^2

5. Which rectangular number is shown by the given dot pattern?

6. (a) Draw a dot pattern to show the number 25.
   (b) Is 25 a square number or a triangular number?

7. Show the triangular number 21 as a dot pattern.

8. Which square number lies between 40 and 50?

9. Which triangular number lies between 40 and 50?

10. Copy the sequences and fill in the missing numbers:
(a) 3, 9, 15, 21, 27, ?, 39, ?, 51, ...
(b) 2, 4, 8, 14, ?, 32, 44, ?, 74, 92, ...

Phase Test 13 → 18

1. Here is a set of numbers:
$\{^-2,\ ^-15,\ ^+6,\ ^-1,\ ^+1,\ ^+24,\ ^-25,\ ^-20,\ ^-5,\ 0\}$
(a) Which is the second smallest number?
(b) Which numbers in the set are less than $^-6$?

2. You may use the number line on p. 69 to help with these if you wish:
(a) $^+6 - 19$ (c) $^-8 - 11$
(b) $^-6 + 19$ (d) $^-5 - 12 + 4$

3. Write these numbers in order of size. Put the smallest first.
$^-8,\ ^-12,\ 0,\ ^+6,\ ^-3,\ ^+1,\ ^-1$

4. Copy and complete the mapping diagram to show supplementary angles.

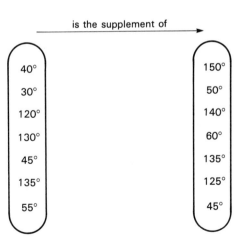

is the supplement of

40°	150°
30°	50°
120°	140°
130°	60°
45°	135°
135°	125°
55°	45°

5. If $x = 8$, find the value of:
(a) $x + 7$ (b) $x - 10$ (c) $2x$ (d) $3x - 5$

6. (*a*) Copy and complete the mapping diagram for the relation 'is 5 less than'.

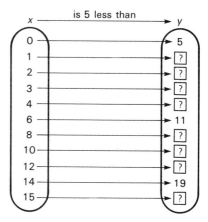

(*b*) Draw a pair of axes as shown.
Use a scale of 1 cm to 1 unit on both axes.
Now draw the graph of the relation 'is 5 less than'.

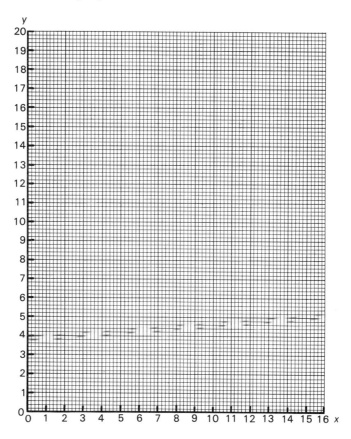

7. The diameter of a bicycle wheel is 65 cm.
   (a) What is the circumference of the wheel?
   (b) How far will the bicycle go if the wheel makes 100 turns?

8. Copy the given shapes on to squared paper. For each
   question, draw the image.
   (a) Shape A is translated 9 units downwards.
   (b) Shape B is reflected in mirror line m.
   (c) Shape C is reflected in mirror line n.
   (d) Shape D is translated 8 units to the right.

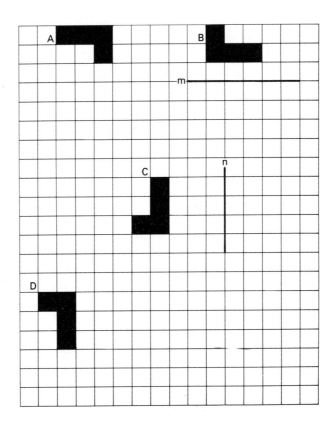

9. Use a calculator to find the value of:
   (a) 2.1^2 (b) 72.5^2 (c) 0.56^2

10. Draw a dot pattern to show the square number 16.

11. Draw a dot pattern to show the triangular number 15.

12. Find the missing numbers in the sequence:

4, 9, 14, ? , ? , 29, 34, 39, ...

Phase Test 19 ════════════════════ Basic Algebra

1. To change centimetres into millimetres, multiply by 10.
Change into millimetres:
(*a*) 5 cm   (*b*) 9 cm   (*c*) 16 cm

2. metres $\xrightarrow{\times 1000}$ millimetres

Change to millimetres:
(*a*) 2 m   (*b*) 7 m   (*c*) 9 m

3. $A = bh$ gives the area of a parallelogram. Find A when $b = 26$ and $h = 7$.

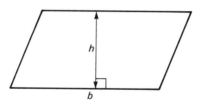

4. Find the value of:
(*a*) $3 \times 5 + 6$ (*b*) $10 - 2 \times 4$

5. If $x = 6$, $y = 2$ and $z = 3$, find the value of:
(*a*) $x + z$ (*b*) xy (*c*) $xz + y$ (*d*) $x - yz$

6. If $p * q$ means $2p + q$, find the value of:
(*a*) $4 * 5$ (*b*) $3 * 9$

7. Simplify:
(*a*) $5l - 2l + 7l - 5l + 2l - l$
(*b*) $4d + 6e - 2e + 6d - 3d + 5e - 5e$

8. Lynn bought $8h$ envelopes. She used $2h$, bought $4h$ then used $5h$.

(a) How many did she have left?

(b) How many did she have left if $h = 5$?

9. Simplify $6 \times 2m$.

10. (a) Simplify $8 \times 7d$.

(b) Find the value of $8 \times 7d$ when $d = 2$.

Phase Test 20 ━━━━━━━━━━━━━━━━━━━━ Statistics

1. The pictogram shows the number of pupils in certain classes who play the guitar:

Number of Pupils who Play the Guitar

(a) How many pupils from class 3 play the guitar?

(b) How many pupils from class 4 play the guitar?

(c) Which class has the most pupils who play the guitar?

2. (a) Copy this tally chart:

Number of pupils	Tally	Frequency
0		
1		
2		
3		
4		
5		

(b) Here is a list of pupils absent last Friday from each class in a school:

$$1 \quad 2 \quad 0 \quad 1 \quad 0 \quad 1 \quad 1 \quad 2 \quad 4 \quad 2$$
$$0 \quad 2 \quad 2 \quad 0 \quad 0 \quad 3 \quad 2 \quad 0 \quad 2 \quad 5$$
$$4 \quad 1 \quad 3 \quad 4 \quad 1 \quad 0 \quad 0 \quad 1 \quad 0 \quad 2$$

Complete your tally chart using the figures given above.

(c) Now draw a bar chart to show the absences.

(First draw a pair of axes as shown below. Use a scale of 2 cm to 1 for the frequency column. Note that one column of the graph has been given.)

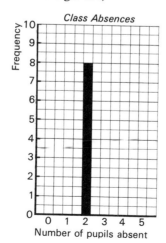

81

3. The jagged line graph shows petrol sales for a week:

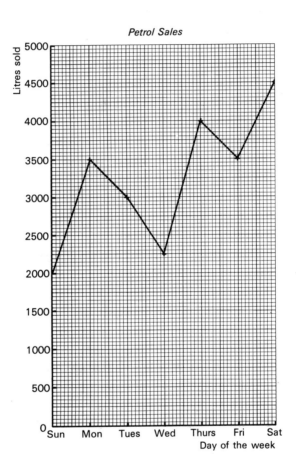

(a) How many litres of petrol were sold on Friday?
(b) On which day were 4000 litres sold?
(c) How many litres were sold on Sunday?
(d) On which days were sales the same?
(e) How many litres were sold on Wednesday?

4. Part of a pie chart has been drawn.
Copy and complete it.

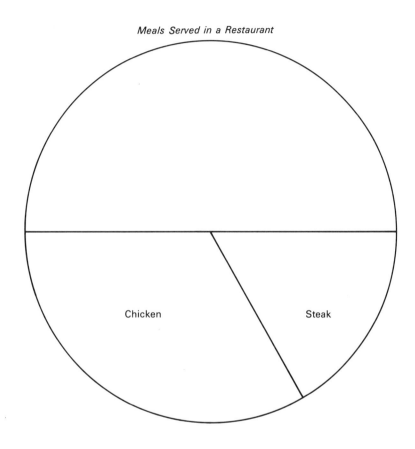

Meals Served in a Restaurant

Chicken

Steak

Meal	Number of people	Angle to be drawn
chicken	12	120°
steak	6	60°
lamb chops	9	
roast beef	3	
plaice	6	

5. In tossing a coin:
if you are more likely to get a head than a tail, write H;
if you are more likely to get a tail than a head, write T;
if a head and a tail have an equal chance, write E.

6. Using the digits 4, 6 and 9 once only in each number,
(*a*) Make as many different 3-digit numbers as you can,
(*b*) Make as many different 2-digit numbers as you can.

Phase Test 21 ━━━━━━━━━━━━━━ Simple Equations

1. Find the value of:
(*a*) $79 + 46 - 46$ (*b*) $82 - 54 + 54$

2. Simplify:
(*a*) $k - 21 + 21$ (*b*) $5y + 4 - 4$

3. Copy and complete:
(*a*) $t + 8 - \boxed{?} = t$ (*b*) $3g - 12 + \boxed{?} = 3g$

4. Copy and complete:

(*a*) $x + 4 \xrightarrow{\boxed{?}} x$ (*b*) $y - 12 \xrightarrow{\boxed{?}} y$

5. Solve these equations:
(*a*) $n + 9 = 16$ (*b*) $p - 7 = 12$

6. Does $v + 16 = 31$ when $v = 15$?

7. Does $8w = 54$ when $w = 7$?

8. Solve these equations:
(*a*) $3l = 24$ (*b*) $6m = 54$

Phase Test 22 ━━━━━━ Length, Capacity and Mass

1. Calculate the perimeter of a rhombus with sides 28 mm.

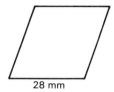

28 mm

2. Construct a parallelogram with one side twice as long as another if the long sides measure 40 mm and an angle between two sides is 70°.

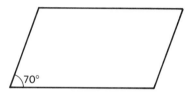

70°

3. A length of cable is 6 ft 4 in. How many inches is that? (12 in = 1 ft.)

4. Change 8.5 ℓ to millilitres.

5. How many pints are there in 3 gal? (8 pt = 1 gal.)

6. A garden watering-can holds:
   A. 1 ℓ   B. 2 ℓ   C. 9 ℓ   D. 30 ℓ

7. Mr and Mrs Davis use 5 ℓ of water every time they wash up.
   (a) How many litres do they use in a day if they wash up three times?
   (b) How many litres do they use in a week if they wash up three times each weekday but four times on Saturday and on Sunday?

8. The total mass of a small can of beans is 288 g. If the beans weigh 225 g, how heavy is the can?

1. Use the conversion tables on p. 36 to change:
   (a) 7 cm to inches   (c) 30 kg to pounds
   (b) 4 miles to kilometres   (d) 20 gal to litres

2. Use the graph below to change:
   (a) 32 m to yards   (c) 72 yards to metres
   (b) 45 yd to metres   (d) 48 m to yards

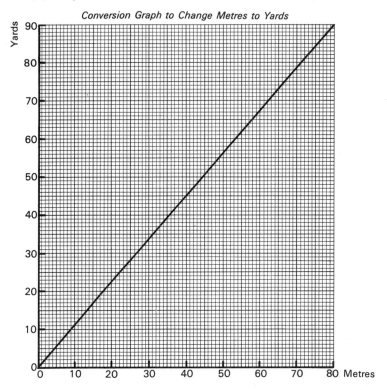

Conversion Graph to Change Metres to Yards

3. Draw a conversion graph to change feet to inches. Use a scale of 2 cm to 1 ft on the horizontal axis and 1 cm to 5 in (2 cm to 10 in) on the vertical axis. (See p. 87.)
   Use 1 ft = 12 in and 8 ft = 96 in.
   Use your graph to change:
   (a) 3 ft to inches   (d) 24 in to feet
   (b) 60 in to feet   (e) 6 ft to inches
   (c) 4 ft to inches   (f) 84 in to feet

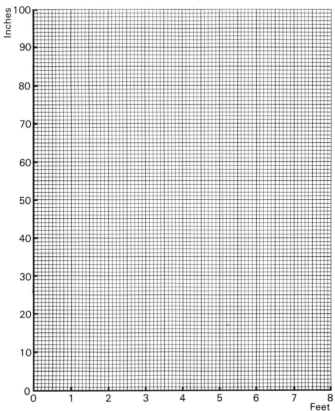

Phase Test 24 ═══════════════════════ Vectors

Use one piece of squared paper throughout this test. Divide it
into four parts as shown on p. 88.

1. On part I of your squared paper, draw 3 separate arrows to
show the vector $\begin{pmatrix} 4 \\ 3 \end{pmatrix}$.

2. On part II of your squared paper, copy the points shown.

(*a*) From A, draw the vector $\begin{pmatrix} 3 \\ 2 \end{pmatrix}$.

(b) From B, draw the vector $\begin{pmatrix} 5 \\ 1 \end{pmatrix}$.

(c) From C, draw the vector $\begin{pmatrix} 1 \\ 2 \end{pmatrix}$.

(d) From D, draw the vector $\begin{pmatrix} 2 \\ 0 \end{pmatrix}$.

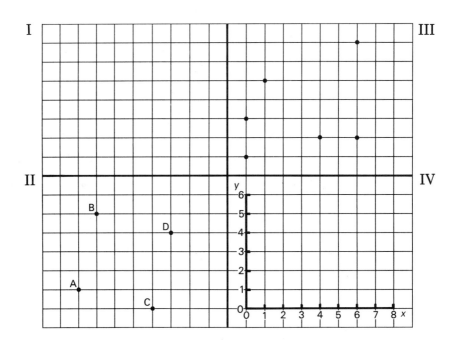

3. On part III of your squared paper, copy the points shown.

(a) Join the two points that show the vector $\begin{pmatrix} 2 \\ 5 \end{pmatrix}$.

(b) Join the two points that show the vector $\begin{pmatrix} 4 \\ 1 \end{pmatrix}$.

(c) Join the two points that show the vector $\begin{pmatrix} 0 \\ 2 \end{pmatrix}$.

4. On part IV of your squared paper draw a pair of axes as shown.

Plot the points R(1, 3), S(2, 1), T(5, 2), U(4, 5), V(4, 0) and W(8, 4).

(a) From R, draw the vector $\begin{pmatrix} 2 \\ 2 \end{pmatrix}$.

(b) From S, draw the vector $\begin{pmatrix} 3 \\ 2 \end{pmatrix}$.

(c) From T, draw the vector $\begin{pmatrix} 2 \\ 1 \end{pmatrix}$.

(d) From U, draw the vector $\begin{pmatrix} 4 \\ 1 \end{pmatrix}$.

(e) From V, draw the vector $\begin{pmatrix} 4 \\ 3 \end{pmatrix}$.

(f) From W, draw the vector $\begin{pmatrix} 0 \\ 2 \end{pmatrix}$.

(Do not forget to draw arrows to show the direction of each vector.)

Phase Test 19 → 24

1. If $c = 4$, $d = 9$ and $e = 3$, find the value of:

   (a) cd (b) $e + d$ (c) $ce - d$ (d) $d - e - c$

2. Simplify $3k + 7l + 4k - 2l - 3k + 4l$.

3. If $g * h$ means $\dfrac{(g + h)}{2}$ find the value of:

   (a) $7 * 5$ (b) $4 * 8$ (c) $9 * 6$ (d) $12 * 0$

4. Draw a bar chart to show the hobbies and pastimes of pupils. Use these results:

Hobby	Number of pupils
reading	4
stamp collecting	5
coin collecting	3
knitting	4
tapestry	2
model making	7
fishing	6
horse riding	2

5. Solve the equation $n - 4 = 18$.

6. Solve the equation $5k = 40$.

7. Does $t + 16 = 40$ when $t = 14$?

8. Does $8m = 64$ when $m = 8$?

9. A rectangular lawn has a length of 21 m. If it has a perimeter of 66 m find its breadth.

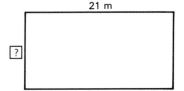

10. A mug holds 250 m*l* and a cup 200 m*l*. How many litres do I need to fill 5 cups and 4 mugs?

11. Find the total mass of a cricket bat weighing 1 kg, a tennis racket weighing 370 g, a cricket ball weighing 160 g and two golf balls weighing 50 g each.

12. Use the conversion tables on p. 36 to change
(a) 7 miles to kilometres
(b) 3 lb to kilograms
(c) 10 in to centimetres
(d) 10 cm to inches
(e) 40 km to miles
(f) 9 gal to litres

13. On squared paper, copy the points shown:

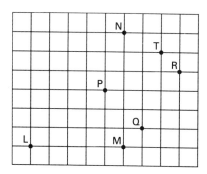

(a) From L, draw the vector $\begin{pmatrix} 2 \\ 4 \end{pmatrix}$.

(b) From M, draw the vector $\begin{pmatrix} 3 \\ 0 \end{pmatrix}$.

14. (a) Write the vector $\overrightarrow{PN}$.

(b) Write the vector $\overrightarrow{LP}$.

15. Join the two points that show the vector $\begin{pmatrix} 2 \\ 3 \end{pmatrix}$.

Phase Test 13 → 24

1. Write $^{+}2$, $^{-}14$, $^{-}6$, $^{+}1$, 0, $^{-}10$, $^{-}7$, $^{-}21$ in order of size. Put the smallest first.

2. You may use the number line on p. 69 to help with these if you wish:
(a) $^{-}3 - 14$
(b) $^{+}3 - 14$
(c) $^{-}18 + 12$
(d) $6 - 15 + 7$

3. Copy and complete the mapping diagram:

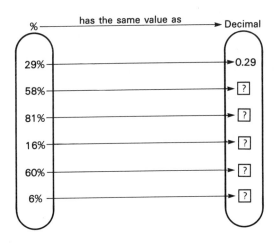

4. Draw a pair of axes as on p. 71.
Answer these questions on the same diagram:
(a) Plot the points A($^-$2, 8), B(3, 8) and C(5, 5).
Join them in that order. Complete parallelogram ABCD.
Write the co-ordinates of D next to vertex D.
(b) Join (4, $^-$2) to (7, $^-$5) to (4, $^-$8) to (1, $^-$5) to (4, $^-$2).
Write the name of the quadrilateral inside the shape.
(c) Join M($^-$7, 0) to N($^-$5, 2) to O(0, 0).
Complete kite MNOP.
Write the co-ordinates of P next to vertex P.

5. The diameter of a bicycle wheel is 49 cm.
(a) What is the circumference of the wheel?
(b) How far will the bicycle go when the wheel makes 10 turns?

6. Copy the shapes shown opposite on to squared paper.
For each question, draw the image:
(a) Shape A is reflected in mirror line m.
(b) Shape B is translated 7 units downwards.
(c) Shape C is reflected in mirror line n.
(d) Shape D is translated 6 units to the right.

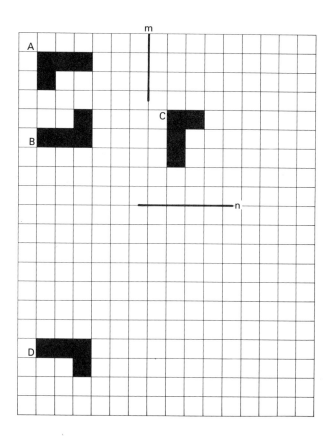

7. Use a calculator to find the value of:
   (a) 8.3^2 (b) 50.2^2 (c) 0.17^2

8. If $f = 9$, $g = 2$ and $h = 12$, find the value of:
   (a) $f + h$ (b) fg (c) $gh - f$ (d) $f - g + h$

9. One side of a parallelogram is twice as long as another. If the shorter sides measure 27 mm, find the perimeter of the parallelogram.

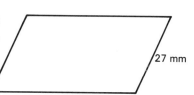

27 mm

10. Solve the equation $c + 13 = 21$.

11. Solve the equation $7w = 42$.

12. The pie chart below shows the number of accidents in November. If the number of accidents in November was 36, find:

(*a*) the number of cars in accidents,

(*b*) the number of motorcycles in accidents,

(*c*) the number of pedestrians in accidents.

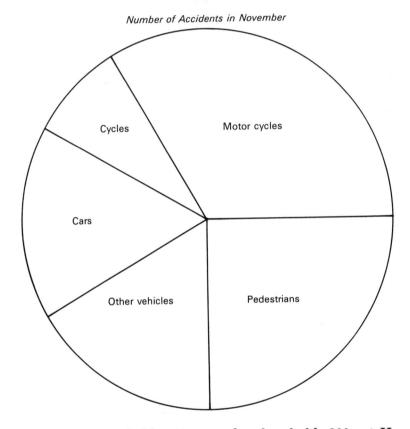

Number of Accidents in November

13. A milk carton holds 500 m*l* and a glass holds 300 m*l*. How many glasses can be filled from 6 cartons?

14. Four apples weigh 520 g. How heavy is one apple if they have equal mass?

15. Use the conversion tables on p. 36 to change:

(*a*) 3 cm to inches   (*c*) 5 *l* to gallons

(*b*) 8 lb to kilograms   (*d*) 30 miles to kilometres

16. (*a*) On squared paper, mark a point J. From J draw an arrow to show the vector

$$\begin{pmatrix} 4 \\ 2 \end{pmatrix}.$$

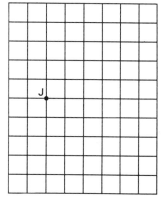

(*b*) On the same piece of squared paper draw two more arrows to show the vector

$$\begin{pmatrix} 4 \\ 2 \end{pmatrix}.$$

(Note: these two arrows may start at any point on your squared paper.)

Phase Test 1 → 24

1. Is the given set an empty set?

{people who were born on 29 February}

2. Answer these:

(*a*)   8237
      + 6968
      ▨▨▨▨

(*b*)   9025
      − 3418
      ▨▨▨▨

(*c*)   8000
      − 2139
      ▨▨▨▨

3. (*a*) Estimate 38×23.

(*b*) In the calculation 38×23 as shown, some digits have been missed out.

```
      3 8
    ×  2 3
    ─────────
    [?] 6 0    20 × 38
  + [?] 1 [?]   3 × 38
    ─────────
    [?][?] 4
    ─────────
```

Copy and complete the calculation.

4. Write B if the given shape
has bilateral symmetry only.
Write R if it has rotational
symmetry only.

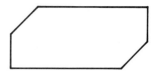

Write BR if it has both bilateral and rotational symmetry.
Write N if it has neither bilateral nor rotational symmetry.

5. Find:

(a) $\dfrac{1}{3}$ of £27   (b) $4 \times \dfrac{2}{3}$ (c) $\dfrac{9}{16} - \dfrac{5}{16}$

6. Calculate the angles labelled θ:

(a)

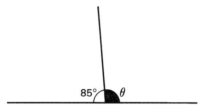

(b)

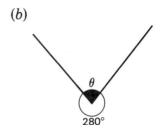

7. Mrs Roberts' lunch cost £4.95 while Mr Hudson paid £2.29 for his lunch. How much more did Mrs Roberts pay?

8. Enlarge the given rectangle.
Make each side twice as long.

9. A patchwork quilt has been
drawn to a scale of 1 cm to 50 cm.
  (a) What is the measured length
    of the quilt in centimetres?
  (b) What is the measured
    breadth of the quilt in centi-
    metres?
  (c) What is the true length of
    the quilt in metres?
  (d) What is the true breadth of
    the quilt in metres?

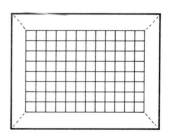

10. Chewing gum packs contain 5 sticks of gum.
How many sticks of chewing gum are there if there are:
(*a*) 2 packs and 1 stick left over?
(*b*) 4 packs and 1 stick left over?

11. Answer these using the timetable on p. 60.
(*a*) If you leave Plymouth at 14.05, at what time do you arrive at Taunton?
(*b*) If you leave Exeter at 20.54, at what time do you arrive at Plymouth?
(*c*) If you arrive at Exeter at 11.04, at what time must you have left Bristol Parkway?
(*d*) If you arrive at Bristol Parkway at 09.22, at what time must you have left Taunton?

12. Calculate the area of the parallelogram shown.

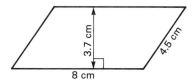

13. Find 50% of £72.

14. You may use the number line on p. 69 to help with these if you wish:
(*a*) ⁻13 – 4   (*b*) ⁻8 + 11   (*c*) 5 – 17   (*d*) ⁻4 + 7 – 13

15. Copy and complete the given mapping diagram:

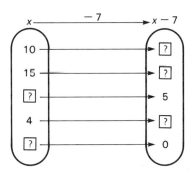

16. Draw a pair of axes as on p. 71. Use a scale of 1 cm to 1 unit on both axes.

(a) Plot and join the points ($^-7$, $^-8$) and (3, $^-4$). What are the co-ordinates of the mid-point of the straight line joining the two points?

(b) Plot the points A($^-2$, 4), B(6, 4) and C(4, $^-2$). Join them in that order. Find a point D such that ABCD is a parallelogram.
What are the co-ordinates of D?

17. The diameter of a paint tin is 90 mm. What is the circumference of the tin?

18. If the given shape is rotated through $\frac{1}{4}$ turn anticlockwise, draw the image position.

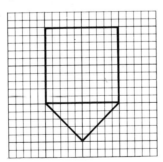

19. Find the value of 11^2.

20. To change gallons into pints, multiply by 8.
How many pints are there in:

(a) 3 gal?   (b) 7 gal?   (c) 19 gal?

21. Pupils were asked for the name of the sport they liked to watch. Here are the results:

Sport	Number of pupils
cricket	4
football	7
netball	5
hockey	6
tennis	8
basketball	7

Draw a bar chart to show these results.
Use a scale of 2 cm to stand for 1 person.

22. Solve the equation $x + 8 = 17$.

23. Solve the equation $6x = 48$.

24. Construct an equilateral triangle with sides of 40 mm.

25. A glass holds 300 ml. How many glasses can be filled from 1.5 l?

26. Find the total mass of a jar of jam weighing 680 g, a jar of coffee weighing 670 g, a packet of flour weighing 1.5 kg and a jelly weighing 135 g.

27. Use the conversion tables on p. 36 to change:
(*a*) 6 in to centimetres
(*b*) 4 km to miles
(*c*) 20 lb to kilograms
(*d*) 40 l to gallons

28. Use the conversion graph below to change:
  (*a*) 20 in to centimetres
  (*b*) 30 in to centimetres
  (*c*) 25 cm to inches
  (*d*) 60 cm to inches

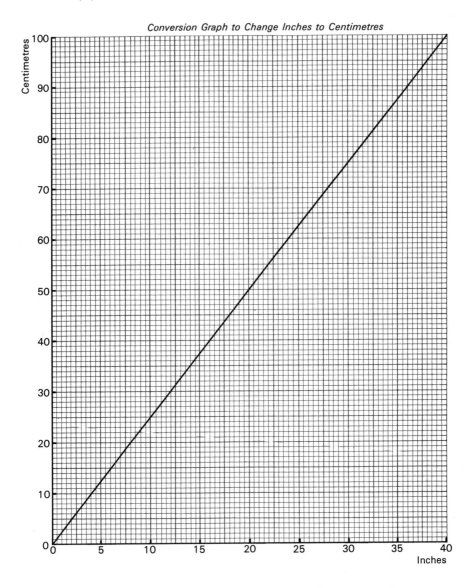

Conversion Graph to Change Inches to Centimetres

29. On squared paper, copy the points shown:

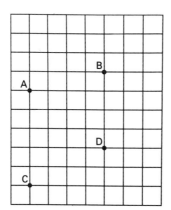

(a) From A, draw the vector $\begin{pmatrix} 3 \\ 2 \end{pmatrix}$.

(b) From B, draw the vector $\begin{pmatrix} 2 \\ 1 \end{pmatrix}$.

(c) From C, draw the vector $\begin{pmatrix} 1 \\ 3 \end{pmatrix}$.

(d) From D, draw the vector $\begin{pmatrix} 2 \\ 0 \end{pmatrix}$.

30. In the diagram above, vector $\overrightarrow{AB} = \begin{pmatrix} 4 \\ 1 \end{pmatrix}$.

Write the vector:

(a) $\overrightarrow{CD}$ (b) $\overrightarrow{CB}$ (c) $\overrightarrow{DB}$